The Mystery of Life

The Mystery of Life

Robert C. Frost, Ph.D.

Distributed by
**Logos International
Plainfield, New Jersey**

Unless otherwise indicated, all Scripture quotations are from the King James Version.

Old Testament Scripture quotations identified by AMPLIFIED are from AMPLIFIED BIBLE, OLD TESTAMENT, Copyright © 1962, 1964 by Zondervan Publishing House, and are used by permission.

New Testament Scripture quotations identified by AMPLIFIED are from The Amplified New Testament © The Lockman Foundation 1958, and are used by permission.

Scripture quotations identified by NAS are from the New American Standard Bible, Copyright © The Lockman Foundation 1960, 1962, 1963, 1968, 1971, and are used by permission.

Scripture quotations identified LB are from The Living Bible, Copyright © 1971 by Tyndale House Publishers, Wheaton, Illinois 60187. All rights reserved.

Scripture quotations identified as Phillips are from LETTERS TO YOUNG CHURCHES by J.B. Phillips. Copyright © 1947, 1957 by Macmillan Publishing Company, Inc., renewed 1975 by J.B. Phillips. Copyright © 1968 by J.B. Phillips. Used by permission.

The Mystery of Life was formerly published as *The Biology of the Holy Spirit.*

THE MYSTERY OF LIFE
Copyright © 1981 by Robert C. Frost, Ph.D.
All rights reserved
Printed in the United States of America
International Standard Book Number: 0-88270-512-1
Library of Congress Catalog Card Number: 81-80616
Distributed by Logos International, Plainfield, New Jersey 07060

TO Fred and Ruth Waugh
whose prayers and friendship have
been a personal source of encouragement
and inspiration over the years.

Contents

	Preface	9
1	Life's Basic Questions	11
2	The Why of Life	19
3	The Who of Life	39
4	The When of Life	68
5	The Where of Life	89
6	The What of Life	111
7	The How of Life	137

Preface

"But now ask the beasts, and let them teach you;
And the birds of the heavens, and let them tell you.
"Or speak to the earth, and let it teach you;
And let the fish of the sea declare to you.
"Who among all these does not know
That the hand of the LORD has done this,
In whose hand is the life of every living thing,
And the breath of all mankind?"

Job 12:7–10 NAS

As the first naturalists, Adam and Eve must have viewed the wonder of their newly created world with intense interest. Nature became a living laboratory from which many spiritual lessons were to be learned. All Creation declared the glory of God, and thereby pointed to the divine purpose for its existence—and theirs!

Failing the "tree-test" for loyalty, mankind lost his way with God, and with his world came under the curse of sin. In spite of the harshness which evil brought to the earthly realm, something of nature's original beauty and holy purpose still remains for those who seek to find the fingerprints of God upon the face of His Creation. The world of life is a window through which the light of divine truth can enter our hearts and minds to brighten our lives for His glory.

Surely many of the spiritual lessons which Jesus drew from the natural realm of life were learned when as a small boy He climbed the flower-spangled hills near His hometown of Nazareth. It was here that He first considered the ravens which neither sow nor reap; the lilies which neither toil nor spin; and the little sparrow whose fall is noticed by our Heavenly Father. It is not unexpected, therefore, that during the later years of His ministry, a flock of sheep, a harvest field of wheat, or a nearby vineyard would become opportunities for the Master to teach His disciples concerning divine purpose and principles.

Life has never lost its power to present heavenly insights to those who wish to sit and learn at the feet of their Lord. Through the ministry of the Holy Spirit, the Master-Teacher beckons us to follow Him along the pathway of living truth that we might joyfully discover that He Himself is the answer to all of life's questions. That is the reason this little book was written.

ROBERT C. FROST

1
Life's Basic Questions

Some years ago when our youngest daughter was quite small, she came running into the house full of excitement and exclaimed, "Oh, Daddy! Come quickly, please hurry. I found a little fuzzy stick on the ground, and when you poke it, it wiggles!" I responded with what I hoped in her eyes was obvious enthusiasm, and together on our hands and knees we explored the wonders of her new discovery—a long, brightly colored, very fuzzy caterpillar, which indeed would oblige with most delightful "wiggles" when so encouraged by the hesitant hand of a budding biologist.

Since that day our home (maybe zoo is a better word) has been a haven for an endless succession of helpless creatures who, whether they needed it or not, became the objects of great love and attention. (Including a frog in Grandma's bed during one of her periodic visits!) I am sure Brother Noah and I will have much to share when that glad day of heavenly fellowship finally arrives.

The Wonder and Mystery of Life

Yes, life is fascinating! There is a wonder and a mystery to living things which attracts our attention in a peculiar way. Actually, wonder is only a step away from worship. Many times in my own professional studies in biology I have been lifted to a place of praise to God following some new insight or discovery which to me was fantastically beautiful. Indeed the wonders of this world and life were divinely designed to produce praise in the heart of man. Worship to be fully satisfying to God must be personal, purposeful, and freely offered. Of all His creatures only man can consciously and spontaneously praise his Maker for the majesty of His Creation and thereby fulfill the very purpose of its existence. The grandeur of the starry heavens, the beauty in design of the tiny snowflake, the miracle of a baby's cry all wait upon our worshipful response before divine desire is fully satisfied. Perhaps this is the reason our living world so persistently speaks to something within us concerning that which is spiritual, eternal, and divine.

At its inception, natural life always fills our hearts with such a sense of promise and hope that everyone is attracted in a most irresistible way. A box of squirming puppies or fuzzy kittens still charms us all regardless of our age. There is almost a spiritual quality to the scene of a farmer expectantly gazing across his field in the early spring. Little seeds are awakened by the gentle caress of soft, refreshing showers. Bright green blades are seen stretching towards the sun as they obey the inward law of life to grow and reproduce. It almost seems as if the rhythm of living things is related to a destiny which goes beyond that which can be seen by the natural eye. The ravages of time can rust our structures of steel, rot away our prized possessions, even wear down our mighty mountains, but the stream of life flows relentlessly on—as if moved by an unseen power for some timeless but obscure purpose. Yes, there is a mystery to life which not only attracts, but commands our interest and attention. Life indeed is most fascinating!

Man has been created with a strong spirit of inquiry, which must be satisfied whenever a mystery touches his life. Questions create answer-shaped vacuums within, which demand to be filled. Man is a "knower," and is restless when surrounded by unknowns. When correctly controlled, the question-answer mechanism in man has a fantastic potential for great discoveries. Life's greatest discovery will involve the answer to man's greatest unknown—death! "If a man die, shall he live again?" (Job 14:14). If so, another question arises. How is our life here and now to be related to this new life which is everlasting in character? Our study around the theme of spiritual biology is designed both to raise and answer some of life's most basic questions.

Biology: The Logos of Life

Let us begin by defining the word "biology" as it relates to the natural world of life. The term is derived from two Greek root words, "bios" and "logos". Bios may be translated by the word *life,* while logos is often translated by the term *science* or *study.* Therefore, biology is the science or study of natural life.

Logos, however, has a far richer meaning when used in a philosophical sense. Here it may refer to the totality of thought, comprehension of concept, or ultimate in expression. If we were to choose a more colloquial phrase, perhaps we might translate it as the "big idea"!

In the Greek New Testament, *logos* takes on an even greater and more exciting expression. It is the term translated as "word" in the first chapter of John's Gospel:

In the *beginning* was the "Word" [Logos],
and the "Word" was *with* God,
and the "Word" *was* God. . . .
And the "Word" *became* flesh,
and dwelt among us, and we beheld His glory, glory as of the only begotten from the Father, full of grace and truth.

John 1:1,14 NAS (quotes and italics mine)

From the key words italicized in the above passage, several conclusions can be drawn concerning the nature of the "Word":

Beginning	Preexistent
With	Coexistent
Was	Divine
Became	Human

What a comprehensive "word-picture" is presented concerning the Person of the Lord Jesus Christ. No wonder in John 1:1 He is referred to as the "Word" of life—the Living Logos!

A little background into the Jewish and Greek concepts concerning the use of the term "word" would be meaningful at this point. To the Old Testament Hebrew the spoken word was more than just a sound expressing an idea or a thought; *it actually accomplished something!* The first recorded words spoken by God illustrate the concept: "And God said, Let there be light: and there was light" (Genesis 1:3). The Word of the Lord possesses creative and perfecting power. Here is divine wisdom in action. The Word not only speaks, it works!

The early Greeks attributed the order and design which they perceived in the universe to an underlying reason or mind which they called the "logos." It was the *logos* which brought sense and order to what otherwise would have been a senseless, chaotic world. Here was the integrating principle of the entire cosmos. As the *logos* was deified, man was confronted with God, but it was in an impersonal way. It was this idea of the *logos* which was such a fascinating concept to the Greek philosophers of the first century.

John saw the correlation between Jewish and Greek thought concerning the Word, and it strengthened and enriched his use of the term in his writings. He presents Jesus Christ to us as the Logos of Life through which the wisdom and power of God is personified.

As the Divine Logos, He also speaks to us through the universal language of life about God's love. Here is love expressed in terms we can understand. Indeed, the life and death of Jesus fairly shout to us that God loves us—desperately loves us! When on the cross Jesus cried out with a loud voice, "It is finished" (John 19:30), the full definition of the Logos of Life was accomplished. Divine purpose and power were fully and finally expressed. Nothing can be added to that definition of God's love—it is forever complete!

It took the Living Word Himself to show us the magnitude and power of God's love. He had to come within "touching distance" to man for Divine Love to be both clearly seen and heard. John beautifully expresses this thought in his first epistle:

> Christ was alive when the world began, yet I myself have seen him with my own eyes and listened to him speak. I have touched him with my own hands. He is God's message of Life. This one who is Life from God has been shown to us and we guarantee that we have seen him; I am speaking of Christ, who is eternal Life. He was with the Father and then was shown to us. Again I say, we are telling you about what we ourselves have actually seen and heard, so that you may share the fellowship and the joys we have with the Father and with Jesus Christ his Son. And if you do as I say in this letter, then you, too, will be full of joy, and so will we.
>
> 1 John 1:1–4 LB

No written word from the pen of man could have adequately expressed the deep desire of our Heavenly Father that we each one find his place in the fellowship of God's family. He wants to be with us, and for us to be with Him—forever! This is the reason He who was "with God' came to be a short time "with man" that He might accomplish our redemption. St. Matthew records that His name shall be called "Emmanuel, which being interpreted is, God with us" (Matthew 1:23). What a perfectly beautiful interpretation!

The Holy Scriptures emphatically declare that Jesus Christ is the integrating theme for all existence—the answer to all of life's questions. All of God's creative power and wisdom are expressed in and through His Son. He is the Logos for which the Greek philosophers looked. In this light, listen to these familiar passages from God's Word:

> In many and various ways God spoke of old in the words of the prophets, but in this final age He has spoken to us through His Son, who is the predestined Lord of the universe. Through Him He created the worlds, and reaches of space, and the ages of time. He is the radiance of God's glory and the flawless expression of God's nature. He upholds,

maintains, guides, and propels the universe by His mighty word of power. . . . And He existed before all things, and in Him the universe is united.

Hebrews 1:1–3; Colossians 1:17 (paraphrased)

Only in Jesus Christ can we find the integrating theme which can bring sense and reason to our existence. Truly, He is the key to the mystery of life. Let us further pursue this thought together.

Life's Basic Questions

Natural biology might now be defined as the "word of life" concerning the earthly, temporal realm. Spiritual biology will press beyond these limitations to consider questions related to heavenly and eternal purpose. Since Jesus is the "Word of Life" who can relate the two realms in a way which we can understand, we will expect to find the answers to our questions concerning life as we become better acquainted with Him.

I usually organize my initial survey lecture in freshman biology in an interesting way around the six journalistic questions which are required for a comprehensive investigation. They are as follows: who, what, where, when, how, and why. The first five questions as related to natural biology can be investigated by means of the scientific method. Philosophical "why" questions are beyond the means of science, as are all questions related to moral judgments (good and evil, right and wrong) and ultimate purpose. This sometimes comes as a surprise to those who have always thought all realms of experience are open to scientific investigation.

The "who of life" questions are concerned with the identification and classification of living things. The science of classification is called taxonomy. In the spiritual realm we also have important questions concerning identity. Who am I? Who is my brother? Who is God? Who is the Holy Spirit? Who is Satan and his hosts? Proper identification is essential. Mistaken—or lack of—identity can be serious.

The "what of life" questions define the characteristics of life. What are the characteristics of living things which distinguish them from dead (once living) or nonliving (physical) things? What structures and functions are common to all living forms? What are the characteristics of being spiritually alive? What is missing in someone who is spiritually dead? What indeed is spiritual life? Death?

The "where of life" questions deal with the relationship of living things to their environment. This field of study is called ecology. How do living things affect their environment? How does environment influence living things? Are there interdependent relationships in life which are so delicately balanced that any sudden change would result in death? What about the pollution problem? Spiritual parallels immediately come to mind, and a corresponding study of spiritual ecology would be intensely interesting!

The "when of life" questions deal with the timing, rhythms, and cycles of life. Does life involve a necessary sequencing and synchrony of events for life cycles to complete themselves? Is the same timing necessary in spiritual growth and development? Can a hasty or lazy spirit in our lives throw us out of step with God's purpose and power? Is there a spiritual rhythm with which we are to be in harmony?

The "how of life" questions are concerned with the energy requirements of living things. What is the source and pathway of transfer for the motivating force for life? Are there diseases that are related to low-energy levels in the cells, tissues, and organs? What is the ultimate source of spiritual power? Is it possible to be spiritually anemic, and is there a cure? Do we hold to a form of godly life, but deny the full expression of its power?

The "why of life" question touches on the very purpose of our existence. Why are we alive? Is there any eternal meaning to our existence? Where did we come from, and where are we going in an ultimate sense? What is life all about? The expression on the faces of many students indicates some of them have never before really asked themselves this most important of all questions concerning life—their life!

In summary, life's basic questions and related topics may be outlined as follows:

> WHY: The meaning or purpose of life
> WHO: The identification or classification of life
> WHAT: The characteristics or qualities of life
> WHERE: The ecology or environment of life
> WHEN: The cycles or rhythms of life
> HOW: The energy or power of life.

Jesus Christ: The Logos of Life

One cannot have purpose without its first being sourced in personality. Divine purpose, therefore, requires a divine personality for its expression. For these reasons, in the chapters that follow we shall turn to the Lord Jesus Christ, who *is* the "Logos of Life," that we might find The Answer to the basic questions which have been raised. As the Apostle Paul so precisely yet powerfully expressed it, He is the ultimate source for all the answers of life—now and forever!

> All things were created by Him and for Him: He was before all else began, and in Him all things consist, cohere, and are integrated into a harmonious whole . . . In Him are hidden all of the treasures of divine wisdom and insight. . . . He is the Source, Guide, and Goal of all that is—to whom be glory forever.
> Colossians 1:16,17 and 2:3; Romans 11:36 (paraphrased)

2
The Why of Life

The answer to the "why" question concerning life is the pivotal point around which all of the other questions and answers find their proper perspective and position. To put it another way, the wheel of life contains a rim, hub, and five connecting spokes. The rim represents the natural, temporal, and earthly aspects of existence. The hub corresponds to the spiritual, eternal, and heavenly purpose for life. The "why" of life can only be found at the center of the wheel. The spokes represent practical and personal answers to the remaining who, how, what, when, and where questions concerning life and are the effective means of relating the center to the periphery.

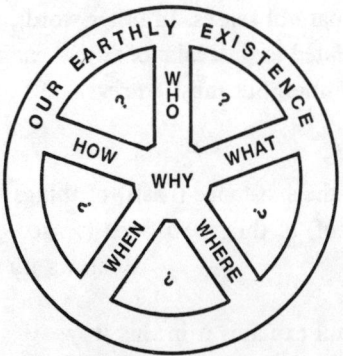

THE WHEEL OF LIFE

The power and purpose of the axle can only be effectively transmitted to the rim (where the rubber meets the road) by way of the spokes.

The answers to life's questions are to be personified through God's people. We are the spokes in the wheel and the only means God has chosen through which His will is to be achieved here on earth as it is in heaven.

Divine answers are always alive. The greatest answer God ever gave was through the life of His Son. As He was sent of the Father, so the Lord Himself has sent us. We are not only to find the answers to life, but to be the answers to life!

Our study now moves from something of academic interest and curiosity to that which is both very personal and practical. We will pursue our theme together by beginning at the center of the wheel and considering the "why" of life.

Limitations of Science and Philosophy

Since biology is the science of life, one might assume the scientific method could cover the entire range of basic questions posed earlier. It is a method of inquiry and designed to discover many of the secrets of natural life. The realm of science, however, has limitations and is related only to areas of life experience which can be perceived and measured by our natural senses. In other words, spiritual truth and life—which are related to the realm of faith—cannot be "sensed out" by our natural abilities, but must be revealed by and received from God.

> Now faith is the substance (basis) of things hoped for, the evidence (proof) of things *not* seen (sensed out).
> Hebrews 11:1 (paraphrased)

The Apostle Paul explains it in this way:

> Eye has not seen and ear has not heard nor has it entered into the heart of man the things which God has prepared for those that love Him. But God has revealed them to us by

His Spirit. . . . But the natural man does not receive the things of the Spirit of God, for they are nonsense to him, because they are appreciated only by spiritual insight.

1 Corinthians 2:9, 10, 14 (paraphrased)

You won't find God on the other end of a telescope unless He has first been found in your heart. This is the simple explanation for the statement by the Soviet astronaut who claimed he had not met God in outer space. We won't see much of God on the outside until we have received Him on the inside!

Furthermore, there are no purpose- or value-revealing steps in the scientific procedure. Science has discovered the power of the atom, but it can not judge the rightness or wrongness of how and where that power is to be released. It is not that kind of yardstick. You cannot measure the room temperature with a twelve-inch ruler. Likewise, the meaning and purpose of life will never be found in a test tube; such answers range far beyond the limitations of the scientific method.

The Scripture quotation above also clearly indicates that divine purpose cannot be "reasoned out" by the means of philosophy; the mind of man is an island of ideas which is bound by that which is earthly and temporal. It takes the lifting power of God's Spirit to launch us into the heavenlies whereby we can gain an eternal perspective and discover the spiritual meaning of our existence. The Apostle Paul reinforces this truth in the following passage:

I will destroy the wisdom of the wise and bring the philosophy of the philosophers to naught. Where is the scholar and the investigator of this age? Has not God made foolish the philosophy of the world? For when the world in its wisdom failed to find God, God was pleased through the foolishness of preaching (Paul's spiritual revelation of Christ) to save those who would put their faith in Him.

1 Corinthians 1:19–21 (paraphrased)

The outline following summarizes our discussion concerning the limitations of science and philosophy.

MEANS AND METHODS FOR DISCOVERING ETERNAL PURPOSE

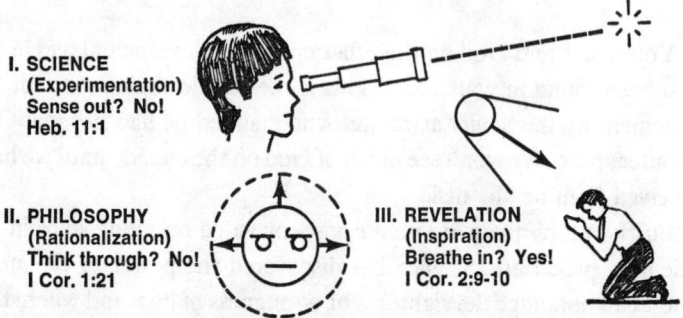

I. SCIENCE
(Experimentation)
Sense out? No!
Heb. 11:1

II. PHILOSOPHY
(Rationalization)
Think through? No!
I Cor. 1:21

III. REVELATION
(Inspiration)
Breathe in? Yes!
I Cor. 2:9-10

There are two interesting passages in the New Testament concerning men who reached the heights of heaven and thereby actually broke through the time barrier into the wonders of the eternal dimension. Their descriptions of the experience emphasize how limited are the perceptive powers of men who, apart from God's Spirit, are prisoners of time, space, and matter. Listen carefully to these words of the Apostle Paul:

> Fourteen years ago I was taken up to heaven for a visit. Don't ask me whether my body was there or just my spirit, for I don't know; only God can answer that. But anyway, there I was in paradise, and heard things so astounding that they are beyond a man's power to describe or put in words (and anyway I am not allowed to tell them to others).
>
> 2 Corinthians 12:2–4 LB

The Apostle John records his amazing experience as follows:

> Then as I looked, I saw a door standing open in heaven, and the same voice I had heard before, that sounded like a

mighty trumpet blast, spoke to me and said, "Come up here and I will show you what must happen in the future!" And instantly I was, in spirit, there in heaven and saw—oh, the glory of it!—a throne and someone sitting on it!

Revelation 4:1,2 LB

Eternal Purpose Requires a Spiritual Revelation

What Paul heard and John saw in the Spirit were divine mysteries concerning the eternal purpose and heart-desire of our Heavenly Father. Earthly words are weak and inadequate vehicles to convey such a mighty message to the mind of man. Language is born from the experience of man with his world. Apart from God, man's life is limited to his awareness of temporal, earthly things. Spiritual truth, heavenly and eternal realities are beyond the limits of his world—and his language! Both of the apostles in their writings concerning spiritual mysteries are forced to fall back upon the use of metaphors and symbolic speech in their endeavor to help us understand the wonder of God's wisdom and will as it is to touch our lives here on earth in time! Both men realized it would take the revealing power of God's Holy Spirit to translate spiritual truth into the language of our daily lives.

There is a heavenly echo to all of Paul's writings, and most clearly can it be heard in this portion of his first letter to the young Corinthian Christians:

> I do speak words of great wisdom to those who are spiritually mature, but not a wisdom belonging to this passing age, nor to any of its governing powers which are declining to their end; I speak God's hidden wisdom, His secret purpose framed from the beginning of time to bring us to our full glory. The powers that rule this world have never known it; if they had, they would not have crucified the Lord of glory. But in the words of Scripture, "Things beyond our seeing,

things beyond our hearing, things beyond our imagining, God has prepared for those who love Him!" Furthermore, He has, through the Spirit, shared His secret with us. For the Spirit searches out and shows us even the depths of God's own nature. No one can really know what anyone else is thinking, or what he is really like, except that person himself. And no one can know God's thoughts except God's own Spirit. God has actually given us His Spirit and not the spirit of the world, that we may know all that God of His own grace gives us, and because we are interpreting spiritual truths to those who have the Spirit, we speak of these gifts of God in words found for us not by our human wisdom but by the Spirit.

1 Corinthians 2:6–13 (paraphrased)

I have noticed when participating in meetings as a speaker in foreign lands that a truly effective interpreter endeavors to convey both the thought and the feeling of the speaker to the audience. God always speaks to us both from His understanding and His affection. The Holy Spirit as our faithful interpreter will likewise always seek to reach not only our minds but our hearts as well. Only a genuine heart-knowledge of God can really satisfy both the rational and emotional needs of man. Divine truth not only stimulates our thinking, but stirs our affections as well.

There are mysteries in God's will and divine purpose which can be perceived only by the inner eye and ear of man's spirit and soul. The pursuit of truth is a high and holy adventure which brings a heavenly freshness to our earthly existence. There is a holy excitement to eternal life which only men and women of the Spirit can experience. One can sense the intensity of feeling which motivated the Apostle Paul as he endeavors through his letters to lift us into the heavenlies upon the wings of words—divinely inspired words.

Breaking the time barrier in both directions, Paul reveals to us the mystery of God's ultimate purpose and pleasure as it was conceived in eternity past and shall be completed in eternity future. Only as the mystery is revealed to us here in time can our lives take on a sense of divine destiny. The writer of Ecclesiastes declares that man has been born with eternity in his heart, and temporal pleasures will never satisfy his longing for the meaning which only divine purpose can bring. No wonder there is a sense of anticipation in Paul's letters as he informs his readers that God has charged him with the pleasure and responsibility of sharing His eternal secrets with us.

So oriented to the eternal is Paul that little phrases like "before the foundation," or "beginning of the world," and "forever"—or more emphatically, "forever and forever"—are sprinkled throughout his writings. (Only St. John in the New Testament is as generous with the latter phrase. It occurs thirteen times in the Book of Revelation.) These are men living within an eternal perspective. Their heavenly vision changed their earthly lives—and it will change ours too!

The Eternal Heart-Desire of the Father

What was it that Paul saw as he peered back through the tunnel of time to its beginning—and then beyond? He was given a view into the very heart of the Eternal Father, and there he beheld the desire of the ages—in the form of His only begotten Son! It was a beautiful love relationship which they shared with one another in the communion of the Holy Spirit.

> . . . I was daily his delight, rejoicing always before him.
> Proverbs 8:30

> . . . for thou lovedst me before the foundation of the world.
> John 17:24

> You are My Son, the Beloved! In You I am well pleased and find delight!
> Luke 3:22 AMPLIFIED

> ... the only unique Son, the only-begotten God, Who is in the bosom ... of the Father ...
>
> John 1:18 AMPLIFIED

The little word "with" in the opening verses of John's Gospel now takes on a weight and a value which we may have overlooked:

> In the beginning was the Word, and the Word was *with* God, and the Word was God.
>
> John 1:1 (Italics mine)

You wouldn't think such a little preposition would carry much meaning (there are over 4,500 "with" words in the Bible). The Greek word for "with" here used refers to a close, intimate, face-to-face, person-to-person, heart-to-heart relationship. The "withness" of this passage speaks of a loving relationship which the Father and the Son through the fellowship of the Holy Spirit have enjoyed from before the beginning of time. The Father has ever found delightful pleasure in His Son; and the will and desire of the Father have always been a joy for the Son to fulfill.

The beautiful communion which they shared together with the Holy Spirit from all eternity past was never broken until that awful hour on the cross when God's only Son cried out from the horrible agony of His soul, "My God, my God, why hast thou forsaken me?" (Matthew 27:46 and Mark 15:34). And He who knew no sin became sin (our sin) that through Him we might become right with God (2 Corinthians 5:21). The Saviour of the world, as the Son of man, experienced the appalling and inevitable conclusion of man's sin—death! Not just death in a physical sense, but the tragic separation from the Father's presence. He who had been with the Father from all eternity was alone in His hour of anguish. There was no other way!

There is a sense in which the Father had lost His only Son, and the Holy Spirit experienced a grief which only God could know. In a very limited way the sorrow of the Father in a heaven silent with sadness is portrayed for us by the very moving passage which describes the grief of King David over the loss of his son. One is gripped by the pathos of the moment:

> And the king was deeply moved, and went up to the chamber over the gate, and wept; and as he went, he said, O my son Absalom, my son, my son Absalom! Would God I had died for you, O Absalom, my son, my son!
> 2 Samuel 18:33 AMPLIFIED

Something of God did die with Jesus on the cross. Herein is tragic mystery of a magnitude which only eternity can reveal. How great was the price for our redemption!

Redemptive grace was in the heart of God before time began. Both the Father and the Son planned in love to recover man's loss, knowing full well what the cost would be. Jesus would be "the Lamb of God slain before the foundation of the world." Salvation is a gift, but it was purchased at great price!

The Reason for Our Redemption

The reason our redemption is so important to God is that it involves the fulfillment of His eternal purpose. Salvation restores to us our place in that purpose. The divine mystery which was revealed to Paul now takes on an even greater interest. What could be so significant to the Father that the whole plan of redemption would be involved in its fulfillment? Blood and tears were a part of the divine purchase! We stand amazed and in great expectation as the great apostle draws back the curtain of time and is prepared to show us our part in God's eternal plan of the ages. Here is the sacred story in his own words:

> For I am a minister of the Church by Divine commission, a commission granted to me for your benefit and for a special purpose: that I might fully declare God's Word—that sacred mystery which up till now has been hidden in every age and every generation, but which is now as clear as daylight to those who love God. They are those to whom God has planned to give a vision of the full wonder and splendour of His secret plan for the sons of men. And the secret is simply this: Christ *in you!* Yes, Christ *in you* bringing with Him the hope of all the glorious things to come.
>
> Colossians 1:25–27 PHILLIPS

What is Paul trying to bring to our understanding by his use of the little phrase "Christ in you"? We marvel that the full sweep of God's eternal purpose could be compressed into three little words! Furthermore, we are filled with wonder to discover we are included in that little phrase. Just as sure as Jesus is there, we are there too—in Him, and He in us! Something supremely significant happened when we invited Christ into our lives as Lord and Saviour. Something got inside of us that the ranges of space and the ages of time cannot encompass! We must pursue this further and the Apostle Paul is ready to lead us on:

> How I long for you to grow more certain in your knowledge and more sure in your grasp of God Himself. May your spiritual experience become richer as you see more and more fully God's great secret, Christ Himself! For it is *in Him,* and in Him alone, that men will find all the treasures of wisdom and knowledge.
>
> Colossians 2:2, 3 PHILLIPS

> Be careful that nobody spoils your faith through intellectualism or high-sounding nonsense. Such stuff is at best founded on men's ideas of the nature of the world, and

disregards Christ! Yet it is in Him that God gives a full and complete expression of Himself (within the physical limits that He set Himself in Christ).

Colossians 2:8–10 PHILLIPS

Now Christ is the visible expression of the invisible God. He existed before creation began, for it was through Him that everything was made, whether spiritual or material, seen or unseen. Through Him, and for Him, also, were created power and dominion, ownership and authority. In fact, every single thing was created through, and for, Him. He is both the First Principle and the Upholding Principle of the whole scheme of creation.

Colossians 1:15–17 PHILLIPS

He is the Head of the body made up of his people—that is, his church—which he began; and he is the Leader of all those who arise from the dead, so that he is first in everything; for God wanted all of himself to be in his Son.

Colossians 1:18, 19 LB

From Him everything comes; through Him everything exists, and in Him everything ends—He is the Source, Guide and Goal of all things. To Him be glory forever. Amen—so be it!

Romans 11:36 (paraphrased)

Having established the centrality, preeminence, and supremacy of the Lord Jesus Christ in language so lofty we are left both breathless and speechless, Paul then defines in a more precise way how we personally are related to God's grand and glorious purpose in His Son. The "Christ in *you*" message also involves each one of us in a most unique, intimate, and individual way. At the same time that we find ourselves in Him, we also find ourselves drawn close to each other in a divine destiny which is shared by us all. We are now using words and touching truth which is far beyond our full comprehension. Again we must turn to the inspired pen of the heavenly minded apostle for additional insight: once more his writing lifts us beyond the limitations of time into the eternal counsel of the Godhead before the foundation of the world. Listen intently to these words:

> Long ago, even before he made the world, God chose us to be his very own, through what Christ would do for us; he decided then to make us holy in his eyes, without a single fault—we who stand before him covered with his love. His unchanging plan has always been to adopt us into his own family by sending Jesus Christ to die for us. And he did this because he wanted to!
>
> Now all praise to God for his wonderful kindness to us and his favor that he has poured out upon us, because we belong to his dearly loved Son. So overflowing is his kindness towards us that he took away all our sins through the blood of his Son, by whom we are saved; and he has showered down upon us the richness of his grace—for how well he understands us and knows what is best for us at all times.
>
> God has told us his secret reason for sending Christ, a plan he decided on in mercy long ago; and this was his purpose: that when the time is ripe he will gather us all together from wherever we are—in heaven or on earth—to be with him in Christ, forever. Moreover, because of what Christ has done we have become gifts to God that he delights in, for as part of God's sovereign plan we were chosen from the beginning to be his, and all things happen just as he decided long ago. God's purpose in this was that we should praise God and give glory to him for doing these mighty things for us, who were the first to trust in Christ.
>
> Ephesians 1:4–12 LB

In this beautiful and moving passage we are quite taken by God's deep desire to have a people with which the life and love of His Son could be shared in a beautiful family relationship. Notice the many references in the above passage which clearly convey this thought to us: God chose us to be His very own through . . . Christ. . . . We (are to) stand before Him covered with His love. . . . His . . . plan has always been to adopt us into His own family by . . . Jesus. . . . We belong to His dearly loved Son. . . . He will gather us all together . . . to be with Him in Christ forever. . . . We have become gifts to God that He delights in. . . . We were chosen from the beginning to be His.

It is as if God the Father found such joy and exquisite delight in the lovely, glorious life of His Son that it was His grand desire to extend that life forever through a great family—a family of many sons and daughters, each one of which in his own unique way would express the ever increasing beauty of their Elder Brother, the Lord Jesus Himself!

This is the reason God created the heavens and the earth; and upon that earth He planted a garden. This is the reason that in that garden paradise He made a man in His own image; and out of that man and to that man He brought a woman. This is the reason He gave them authority over all of Creation and told them to multiply, be fruitful, and fill the whole earth. Fill the whole earth with what? To fill the entire earth with life—God's life!

When God Made Man, He Had Jesus in Mind

When man was made in God's own image he was endowed with a potential to develop and express nothing less than the very character of Christ, Himself. Jesus Christ is the "express image of the invisible God" (Colossians 1:15; Hebrews 1:3). When God made man, He had Jesus in mind! He was after a glorious family who would love God and each other in the same way the Father and Son love one another —through the communion of the Holy Spirit.

As we know, the first family failed in fulfilling the desire of the Father. The serpent deceived them into doubting God's love and disobeying His will and they disinherited themselves from His loving and life-giving purpose for their lives. Spiritual fellowship with God and with each other was broken. God, however, in His grace, never changed His mind about having a people who would love Him as He loved them—because they wanted to! This would be a true love based on faith and obedience. The Lord Himself would provide the model and the means for such a recovery.

Only God could have conceived of such a perfect plan—awe-full in its extent but gloriously triumphant! The Lord chose to regain for man the ground he had lost in God's original purpose by becoming a man Himself—what a fantastic scheme!—and by visiting the same earth which had been the setting for such a tragic failure.

Another family is given another chance—and they did not fail, because it was through this family that the Saviour of the world gained entrance to an earth cursed by man's sin. Now God's redemptive plan moves from eternity into time, where lives could be touched by the loving hands of their Elder Brother. Not since the Garden of Eden had there been the same opportunity to walk with God in the cool of the day—once more the Lord was among His people! How the hosts of heaven, lonely from their loss, must have intently watched the divine plan of redemption unfold all the way from a rugged wooden manger to the rugged wooden cross.

I have tried to imagine what a glorious welcome the Lord Jesus must have received following His Ascension and triumphant return to the throne of God. Redemption's plan was now accomplished—the Father's desire for a wonderful family was now ready to be fulfilled. The Son of God had become the Son of man, that the sons of men might become the sons of God! The very thought causes our hearts to well up in praise. The holy angels watched as God poured out His redeeming love through Jesus. But it was our lives that were redeemed!

They Lived Happily Ever After

It is always tempting to look at the last chapter of a mystery book to see how the story ends. The same interest is more than true when the mystery involves our lives and the conclusion involves our eternal destiny. Just imagine how the Apostle John must have felt when he realized he was going to be given the privilege of writing the last chapter in God's Book of divine mysteries! No wonder he says in his introduction to the Book of Revelation:

> Blessed is the man who reads, and happy are those who listen to the words of this prophecy and heed in their hearts what is written in it. For the hour of fulfillment is near!
> Revelation 1:3 (paraphrased)

This seems to imply there is going to be a "they lived happily ever after" conclusion to our story. Is the Father's desire for a family fulfilled? Does God get the people He has persistently pursued with His redeeming love? Do we make the eternal scene? Is this the concluding chapter for our lives as well?

Let us turn to the final pages of God's divine mystery story and discover for ourselves what John was shown and carefully recorded:

> Then I saw a new heaven and a new earth, for the first heaven and the first earth had passed away, and the sea was no more. And I, John, saw the holy city, the new Jerusalem, coming down from God out of heaven. It was a glorious sight, as a bride prepared in beauty for her wedding.

> I heard a great shout from the throne, saying, look, the home of God is now among men, and He will live with them and they will be His people; yes God Himself will be among them and be their God. He will wipe away all tears from their eyes, and there shall be no more death, nor sorrow, nor crying, nor pain. All of that is gone forever!

And the One sitting on the throne said, "See, I am making all things new!" And then He said to me, "Write this down, for these words are trustworthy and true. Indeed," He said, "they are already fulfilled. For I am the Alpha and the Omega, the Beginning and the End. I will give to the thirsty water without price from the fountain of life. He that is victorious and overcomes shall inherit all of these blessings, and I will be a God to him, and he will be a son to Me. But cowards who turn back from following Me, and those who are unfaithful to Me, and the corrupt and the murderers, and the immoral, and those conversing with demons (magic arts), and idol worshippers, and all liars—their doom is in the lake which burns with fire and sulfur. This is the second death!

"Blessed and happy forever are those who wash their robes clean, for they have the right to enter in through the gates of the city and to partake from the Tree of Life."

Revelation 21:1-8 (paraphrased)

Yes, the Father finds His family, and the Son is united forever with His many-membered bride. Just who are the sons? Who all make up the beloved bride of Christ? The Scriptures declare it will be those who together, through God's grace, have overcome the Enemy on his own ground right here in time on earth. Their sonship and related authority are based on their recognizing and receiving Jesus Christ into their lives as Lord and Saviour and subsequently faithfully following the leadership of God's Holy Spirit (John 1:12; Romans 8:13-17).

My, But You Are Peculiar!

The will of the Father is wrapped in His desire to have a people, but not just any people—He wants a "peculiar" people.

> For you are a chosen generation, a royal priesthood, a holy nation, a peculiar people who belong to God, so that you might show forth the praises of Him who called you out of darkness into His wonderful light—you who once were not a people, but now are the people of God.
>
> 1 Peter 2:9, 10 (paraphrased)

The word "peculiar" in modern usage has the connotation of being odd or eccentric. The term in the Greek language, however, has a different and much richer meaning. It actually possesses a trinity of qualities which are encompassed by the words *prized, purchased,* and *possessed.* This insight is reenforced in a similar passage found in Paul's letter to Titus:

> Looking for that blessed hope, and the glorious appearing of the great God and our Saviour Jesus Christ; Who gave himself for us, that he might redeem us from all iniquity, and purify unto himself a peculiar people, zealous of good works.
>
> Titus 2:13, 14

The Greek scholar Kenneth Wuest indicates the word for "peculiar" is a compound term which means "to be surrounded by," as a circle might encompass and thereby possess a central point. In like fashion God's people are in the very center of His will and pleasure! The things of time and earth are at every point, to be surrounded by and subservient to the heavenly circle of God's eternal purpose. What an absolutely amazing prospect!

Paul touches on this in his discussion with the Athenian philosophers at the Areopagus council. Let us listen to his words with the added appreciation the insights above bring to our understanding:

> Then Paul stood in the midst of Mars' hill, and said, Ye men of Athens, I perceive that in all things ye are too supersti-

tious. For as I passed by, and beheld your devotions, I found an altar with this inscription, TO THE UNKNOWN GOD. Whom therefore ye ignorantly worship, him declare I unto you. God that made the world, and all things therein, seeing that he is Lord of heaven and earth, dwelleth not in temples made with hands; Neither is worshipped with men's hands, as though he needed any thing, seeing he giveth to all life, and breath, and all things; And hath made of one blood all nations of men for to dwell on all the face of the earth, and hath determined the times before appointed, and the bounds of their habitation; That they should seek the Lord, if haply they might feel after him, and find him, though he be not far from every one of us: For in him we live, and move, and have our being; as certain also of your own poets have said, For we are also his offspring.

Acts 17:22-28

How exciting it is for God to not only surround us with Himself but desire for us to be aware of His Presence. Some people don't see God in anything; others see Him in everything! It will be our desire in the chapters that follow to allow the Holy Spirit through the witness of God's world and His Word to show us how to live "peculiar" lives for His glory.

Concluding Challenge

In South America they have an interesting proverb which goes something like this: "Keep the center in the middle!" We live in an off-centered, eccentric world, spiritually speaking. Man through sin has missed the center point of God's purpose for his life. The recentralizing power of the Holy Spirit can return us to that place of privilege and responsibility whereby we can connect the heart-desire of the Father from eternity past with its fulfillment in eternity future. The course of God's will must pass through His people here on earth in time. There is no other way. Jesus as our Model Brother has established the pattern and provided the power by sending to us the Holy Spirit of God. He has proved it can be done; and having pioneered the way, He now sends us as the Father sent Him (John 17:18).

We are often cautioned not to be so heavenly minded that we are of no earthly good. Actually, from the divine perspective, unless we are heavenly minded, we cannot be of any earthly good at all as far as God's will is concerned. Only men who have had a vision of the opened heavens know how to move through time with eternity in view. Jesus was such a man; Paul followed in His footsteps, and now we hear his encouraging words to men and women of all ages—"Be ye followers of me, even as I also am of Christ" (1 Corinthians 11:1).

Diagramatic Summary

The following diagram summarizes the purpose of life here on earth in time from a heavenly and eternal perspective.

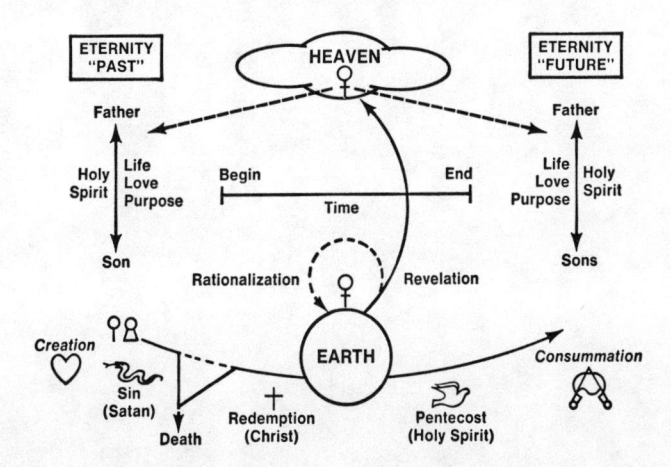

Man is an earth-bound, time-bound, mind-bound creature who cannot by rationalization obtain a heavenly, eternal, or spiritual perspective. Only by the revelation of the Holy Spirit can he discover the eternal heart-desire of the Father to ultimately have a family of many sons like unto their Elder and Redeemer-Brother, the Lord Jesus Christ. A glorious fellowship of life, love, and purpose in the Father's family through the communion of the Holy Spirit is our divine destiny.

3
The Who of Life

Since long before the pigeonhole desk was invented, men have been driven by the desire to bring order out of disorder. "Sifters and sorters" of all ages have persistently sought to compare and categorize what otherwise would have been isolated, unrelated pieces of information. Whether it is the silverware drawer in the kitchen or the book shelves in the neighborhood library, we find items identified by their distinguishing features and grouped together according to the characteristics they share.

The same basic principles apply when it comes to the identification of living organisms. Over the years a highly sophisticated science of classification called "taxonomy" (Greek: *taxis*, arrangement; *nomos*, law) has developed, through which some 335,000 plants and over 1,000,000 animals (800,000 are insects) have been identified. Included in the latter category is man, himself known scientifically by the name of *Homo sapiens*. Yet in the array of life there is none like him in character, for he alone became the crown of Creation—made in the image of God!

Made in the Image of God

God is sovereign; God is unique! Man, therefore, was created with a sovereignty of soul and uniqueness of personality which the Lord God Himself will not violate! Our Heavenly Father will not force His way or will into our lives any more than He did upon His own Son and our divine Elder Brother, the Lord Jesus. There is a mutual respect and "willingness" in love relationships without which personal fulfillment is impossible. The Lord ever honors these qualities of selfhood which by design were fashioned into our lives as individuals from the very beginning. God loves us because He wants to, not because it is forced upon Him; He desires that we love Him in like fashion—because we want to, not because we have to!

I remember in a recent trip through South America the privilege of visiting the "One Minute With God" Community in Bogota, Colombia. It comprises some 10,000 people and 2,000 homes in what otherwise would be an underprivileged area. Father Rafael Garcia-Herreros has gained the respect and love of the people by helping them find a personal dignity through useful service in this unusual Christian community. One evening while we were there some of the young people, who were just being awakened to God's love, dropped in to serenade us. They sat on the floor and played their guitars and sang for us until late in the evening.

We were looking for a natural opportunity to share more personally with them about God's love, and the opening came as we expressed our appreciation for their spontaneous serenade in song. It obviously had been unrehearsed and moved from a genuine desire on their part to please us. We told them we recognized they had come to share with us because they had wanted to, not because they had to. We thanked them for this expression of their love for us and indicated we likewise had come to them because we wanted to. Then we simply related to them how very much God desires for all of us to love each other and to love Him because we choose to do so, for that is exactly how He loves us—because He wants to!

The Holy Spirit melted us together and there was a warm personal display of affection as everyone embraced one another and we joyfully parted for the evening. Something of the freely given love of God, however, remained in all of our hearts.

Man was made to receive and share the eternal life and love of God. Apart from the Lord and His people there is no lasting love to be given and no one with whom it can be shared. Man's purpose in life then is missing, and apart from divine purpose man cannot find himself as a person. Something of this is sensed in the loneliness with which Adam viewed the whole array of living creatures as they were brought before him for his identification. The account as described in the second chapter of Genesis indicates that among them all there was not found for him a suitable helpmate. (The *help meet* in Genesis 2:18 literally means one who *corresponds* and *responds*.) The naming process involved an ability on Adam's part to perceive both corresponding and distinguishing features of all the various animal forms. Nothing was found to which his own person—spiritually, psychologically, or physically—could respond. Something was missing, and that something was someone!

Adam had been created to share God's life and love with another that they together might bring forth a family for the divine pleasure of their Heavenly Father. It was a family that was to live forever united with God and each other through His love. Yet here was Adam viewing the wonders of a beautiful new world—alone!

Purpose and Personality Are Mutually Interdependent

It is impossible to have purpose without personality. It is also impossible to have personality without purpose! Adam's purpose in life was incomplete without his helpmate; likewise, he was incomplete as a total person. He could not discover or define his identity as an individual as long as he remained alone. He could not be himself apart from another. For this reason God, viewing the sadness of the scene, exclaimed, "It is not good for man to dwell alone."

From the side of man there is then brought forth a woman who immediately is recognized as being "bone of my bones and flesh of my flesh." It was in their unity with each other and the Lord that they found their identity as unique individuals. Only God could reveal to them their divine destiny. Only together could that destiny be fulfilled. But it involved the principle of willing submission first to God, then to each other in the roles which the Lord had ordained for them as husband and wife, and father and mother. The earthly horizon indeed was bright with a heavenly hope—save for one shadow, which now falls upon the scene!

In the guise of a graceful serpent an Adversary seeks to spoil God's divine plan for man. He had previously marred the harmony of heaven by introducing the discordant note of rebellion into the angelic hosts. How could the coils of such a sinister scheme come to embrace both the heavenly and earthly creation? The power and intelligence behind such a bold and sweeping move must have been sourced in a most remarkable and unusual personality. Certainly his identification becomes of supreme importance. The Apostle John refers to him as "that old serpent, called the Devil and Satan, which deceiveth the whole world" (Revelation 12:9).

One of Satan's greatest deceptions is to darken men's minds concerning his personal existence and power. Again it is impossible to have purpose without personality; it is also impossible to have evil purpose without evil personality! There are many references in Scripture which ascribe the characteristics of intelligent individuality to Satan. To be deceived into discounting the power and personality of the devil is to open our lives to his influence without knowing it. We will neither defend ourselves against or directly attack an enemy we do not believe exists. This is a rather serious position to assume when Holy Scriptures repeatedly instruct us concerning the reality of our spiritual warfare.

Just as hikers need to know the identifying characteristics and behaviour patterns of poisonous serpents which inhabit the terrain over which they travel, we need to be aware of Satan's presence along our pilgrim pathway. Tree snakes are often green in color, while those which frequent rocky areas are camouflaged by mottled patterns of gray and brown. Satan likewise assumes the color of his surroundings and even masquerades as an "angel of light" when within a religious context (2 Corinthians 11:14, 15).

Fortunately the Holy Bible is an adequate fieldbook regarding the natural history and identifying characteristics of "that old serpent called the Devil and Satan." We can confidently and safely turn to the Scriptures for proved and practical information concerning the character of our adversary, for we are not to be "ignorant of his devices" (2 Corinthians 2:11).

The Origin of Good and Evil

How did the conflict between good and evil begin in the first place? Certainly God did not create evil by design. How was it realized and through whom? There are some passages in Holy Scripture which rather obviously point beyond earthly settings and personalities to the origin of evil in the heavenly realm. We find an unusual individual is involved—one whom the Prophet Ezekiel describes as being supremely beautiful, intelligent, and powerful in God's order of Creation—someone who was in a position of high honor and authority:

> You were the perfection of wisdom and beauty. You were in Eden, the garden of God; your clothing was bejeweled with every precious stone ... all in beautiful settings of finest gold. They were given to you on the day you were created. I appointed you to be the anointed guardian cherub. You had access to the holy mountain of God. You walked among the stones of fire [possible reference to the angels].
>
> You were perfect in all you did from the day you were created until that time when wrong was found in you. Your great wealth filled you with internal turmoil and you sinned ... Your heart was filled with pride because of all your beauty; you corrupted your wisdom for the sake of your splendor.
>
> Ezekiel 28:12–17 LB

The immediate reference in this passage is to the king of Tyre, but the lofty language used obviously relates more accurately to the satanic power behind the king which motivated his earthly actions. A similar passage is found in Isaiah. The king of Babylon is invested with a description which characterizes the evil personality which possessed his life. Again the basic attitude is that of devilish pride and rebellion:

> How you are fallen from heaven, O Lucifer, son of the morning! How you are cut down to the ground—mighty though you were against the nations of the world. For you said to yourself, "I will ascend to heaven and rule the angels. I will take the highest throne. I will preside on the Mount of Assembly far away in the north. I will climb to the highest heavens and be like the Most High." But instead, you will be brought down to the pit of hell, down to its lowest depths.
> Isaiah 14:12–15 LB

It would appear that the angelic beings that comprised the heavenly host were created as moral personalities. They were endowed with a degree of individual sovereignty which allowed them the privilege of choice in regard to their loyalty and love for God. Once more we are reminded that true love can never be programmed or forced, for inherent in its nature is the quality of personal freedom. The little words "I love you" would lose their beauty and value if they did not arise spontaneously from a willing heart. Real love must be freely given! God loves us because He *chose* to create us as objects of His love. He didn't have to express His love in this way, but He wanted to. He desires that we likewise choose to love and trust Him because we want to, not because as "divine robots" we have no other alternative.

Wherever there is the freedom of choice, there is the risk of rejection and the consequences that rejection might bring to all concerned. To reject divine love, truth, and goodness is to realize the potential for hatred, error, and evil. You cannot flip a one-sided coin; for every "heads" there is the possibility of the opposite side called "tails."

The Devil's Delusion

That Satan made the wrong choice is obvious. That hatred, error, and evil were actualized as a consequence of that decision is without dispute. How the devil was deceived into thinking he could get away with his rebellion requires some reflection, however. The Scriptures declare he was the "perfection of wisdom." Furthermore, it was impossible for him to be tempted from "without," because there was no "outside" evil personality to influence his thinking. What could have been the source of his downfall?

The passages from Ezekiel and Isaiah indicate that Satan became infatuated with himself. He found great pleasure in his own beauty. He derived much self-satisfaction from his exalted position of power and authority. His sense of values shifted, and all that seemed really worthwhile became centered in himself. God had indeed placed him in a unique position among the angelic beings. As his perspective changed, however, so did his character and conduct; divine qualities were perverted by the corrupting power of pride:

DIVINE		SELF
Authority	POWER	Assertion
Honor	PRESTIGE	Exhaltation
Satisfaction	PLEASURE	Gratification
Destiny	PURPOSE	Determination
Beauty	PERFECTION	Admiration

Worship is called forth because of the "worthship" of what is worshipped. Satan not only worshipped himself, but sought the worship of the heavenly host. What a contrast to the picture we find in John's account of the Revelation:

> And I beheld, and I heard the voice of many angels round about the throne, and the beasts, and the elders: and the number of them was ten thousand times ten thousand, and

thousands of thousands; Saying with a loud voice, Worthy is the Lamb that was slain to receive power, and riches, and wisdom, and strength, and honour, and glory, and blessing. And every creature which is in heaven, and on the earth, and under the earth, and such as are in the sea, and all that are in them, heard I saying, Blessing, and honour, and glory, and power, be unto him that sitteth upon the throne, and unto the Lamb for ever and ever.

Revelation 5:11–13

How grieved the Holy Spirit must have been as Satan filled his heart with pride and withdrew from worshipping Him who was the Lamb slain from before the foundation of the world (Revelation 13:8). How saddened was the Father to see His Son rejected by one who had been the noblest of His created beings. The ugly stain of sin spread forth before the very throne of God, and an evil shadow was seen within the holy courts of heaven by all of the angelic hosts. Our minds cannot comprehend how intensely horrible and hideous a scene was created as Satan in defiance challenged the Lordship of Jesus Christ.

The Cause and Consequences of Rebellion

An analysis of rebellion may be outlined as follows:

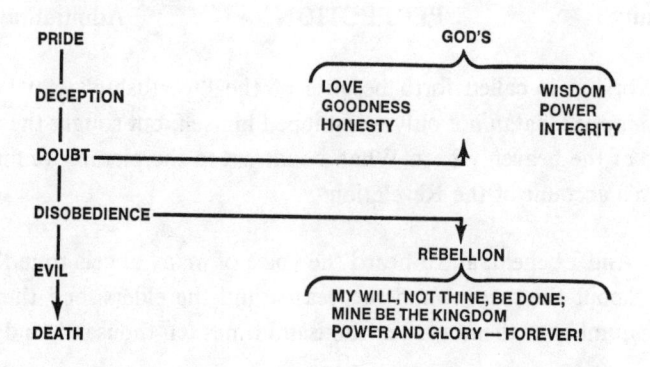

```
PRIDE                          GOD'S
  |                    ┌──────────────────┐
DECEPTION              LOVE        WISDOM
  |                    GOODNESS    POWER
                       HONESTY     INTEGRITY
DOUBT ─────────────────────────▲
  |
DISOBEDIENCE ──────────────┐
  |                        ▼
EVIL                     REBELLION
  |                   ┌──────────────────────────┐
                      MY WILL, NOT THINE, BE DONE;
                      MINE BE THE KINGDOM
DEATH                 POWER AND GLORY — FOREVER!
```

Contained within pride are the elements of delusion; to reject truth is to accept the error of deception:

> An overseer must be blameless . . . self-controlled, self-restrained, disciplined . . . not a novice, lest being puffed up by pride and blinded by conceit, he fall into the condemnation incurred by the devil.
>
> 1 Timothy 3:2–6 (paraphrased)
>
> The coming of the Antichrist will be through the cunning work of Satan with all kinds of deceptive signs and wonders, and all the delusions of unrighteousness for those who are doomed to destruction; because they rejected the truth through which they might have been saved. For this reason, God will send them a strong delusion that they believe a lie with all of their hearts, and consequently be justly judged for refusing the truth and taking pleasure in unrighteousness—wicked disobedience.
>
> 2 Thessalonians 2:9–12 (paraphrased)

Lucifer actually believed his rebellion would prove successful, for one with his wisdom would never have championed a cause obviously destined for defeat. Furthermore, he persuaded many of the heavenly host to join with him (2 Peter 2:4; Jude 6). The most effective deceiver is one who himself is deceived, for he speaks with both sincerity and conviction.

What might have been the basis of such a large-scale defection? As a created being Lucifer had no prior basis on which to measure his identity and importance—only God's Word. He was not omniscient (all knowing) and, therefore, did not foresee the ultimate consequences of his rebellion. Rebellion's power had never before been tested. The results of sin and evil were unknown. Immortal creatures had no concept of death. Furthermore, he may have sought to exploit what he thought was a weakness in God's ultimate plan and purpose!

An overview of Scripture seems to establish that God chose to accomplish His divine intention in Creation through creatures who were given a freedom of will (angels, man). Furthermore, God was committed to the noble proposition that should some of His creatures choose their will and way rather than His, ultimately:

Good		**Evil**
Love	**WOULD**	**Hate**
Light		**Darkness**
Truth	**OVERCOME**	**Error**
Right		**Wrong**

through creatures who would still choose to recognize His Lordship!

Satan sought to challenge that concept, and the conflict between good and evil was realized in a manner that demanded an ultimate conclusion. The relentless war of the ages was under way and becomes the background against which the goodness and grace of God will yet prevail—through a family of loyal and loving sons and daughters!

The Infection Spreads From Heaven to Earth

Adam and Eve had been commissioned by their Heavenly Father to bring forth a royal family whose life was to fill the whole earth with God's glory and power. The entire realm of nature had been placed under their authority and they were to govern the earth with divine purpose in view:

> Then God said, "Let us make a man—someone like ourselves, to be the master of all life upon the earth and in the skies and in the seas." So God made man like his Maker. Like God did God make man; Man and maid did he make them. And God blessed them and told them, "Multiply and fill the earth and subdue it; you are masters of the fish and birds and all the animals. And look! I have given you the

seed-bearing plants throughout the earth, and all the fruit trees for your food. And I've given all the grass and plants to the animals and birds for their food."

Genesis 1:26–30 LB

To the first family there was given a destiny and a dignity. Their identity was established by their commission. The realization of their God-given personalities would be determined by the extent to which they were willingly submitted to the divine purpose for which they had been created. Self-discovery must be preceded by a living self-surrender to the loving will of God. The two go hand in hand and cannot be separated from eternal purpose.

Satan now attempts to infect the first earthly family with the same sickness which was the cause of his own downfall from the heavenly heights—pride and rebellion! He cannot overpower them in his guise as a beautiful serpent, for God has given them authority over all the beasts of the field. He has only one avenue of approach, and that is by the means of deception (2 Corinthians 11:3).

The deception and disobedience of Adam and Eve centered around two trees which were placed within the garden of their lives. One was called the Tree of Life; the other, the Tree of Death (Knowledge):

> And the LORD God planted a garden toward the east, in Eden; and there He placed the man whom He had formed. And out of the ground the LORD God caused to grow every tree that is pleasing to the sight and good for food; the tree of life also in the midst of the garden, and the tree of the knowledge of good and evil. . . . And the LORD God commanded the man, saying, "From any tree of the garden you may eat freely; but from the tree of the knowledge of good and evil you shall not eat, for in the day that you eat from it you shall surely die."
>
> Genesis 2:8, 9, 16, 17 NAS

Hidden within the mystery of the Tree of Life is the Author of Life, Himself—the Lord Jesus Christ. Likewise, hidden within the mystery of the Tree of Death is the author of death—Satan. The first tree produces the fruit of righteousness and all that is related to our life in Christ. The second tree yields the fruit of rebellion and the consequences of a broken relationship with God. The key concepts are summarized in the outline below:

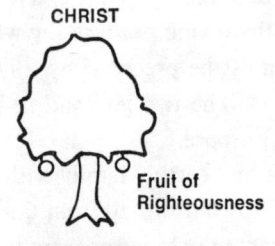

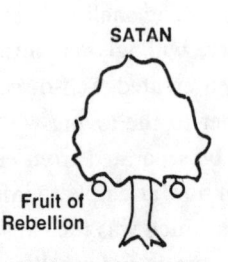

CHRIST — Fruit of Righteousness — TREE OF LIFE

SATAN — Fruit of Rebellion — TREE OF DEATH

TREE OF LIFE	TREE OF DEATH
1. TRUTH: WISDOM OF GOD	1. ERROR: KNOWLEDGE OF MAN
2. OBEDIENCE: *THY* WILL	2. REBELLION: *MY* WILL
3. KINGDOM OF GOD	3. KINGDOM OF SELF (SATAN)
4. MEEKNESS	4. PRIDE
5. DIVINE PERCEPTION	5. SATANIC SELF-DECEPTION
6. FELLOWSHIP	6. ALIENATION
7. IDENTITY—PURPOSE	7. LOSS OF PERSONALITY—PURPOSE
8. FREEDOM—LIBERTY	8. SLAVERY—CAPTIVITY
9. LOVE—JOY—PEACE	9. CONFLICT—SORROW—TURMOIL
10. LIGHT—LIFE	10. DARKNESS—DEATH

The temptation to taste of the forbidden fruit was a challenge to God's love, wisdom, and authority. It was designed to entice them to doubt, then disobey. They were deceived into "thinking" (tree of knowledge) that they could achieve personal destiny and dignity entirely by self-determination: "Be the master of your fate, and the captain of your own soul. You alone decide between what is good and evil; right and wrong; but always in terms of whether it promotes your own personal program or pleasure, power and prestige. You can be yourself, know yourself, and fully express yourself—by yourself. No one else is needed or desired. In this way you will gain all the glory, and become as gods yourself. This is the only way to really live."

The lie worked as well on earth as it had in heaven, and death moved into the history of man. It would have been a timeless tragedy, and the loss not only of man's identity but of the divine purpose which provided that identity, if it hadn't of been for one great redemptive feature—the grace of God! This came as a surprise to Satan, for it was an aspect of God's divine nature in which he was never personally interested.

The Gospel According to Mother Goose

The whole story is vividly presented in one of the familiar Mother Goose Rhymes:

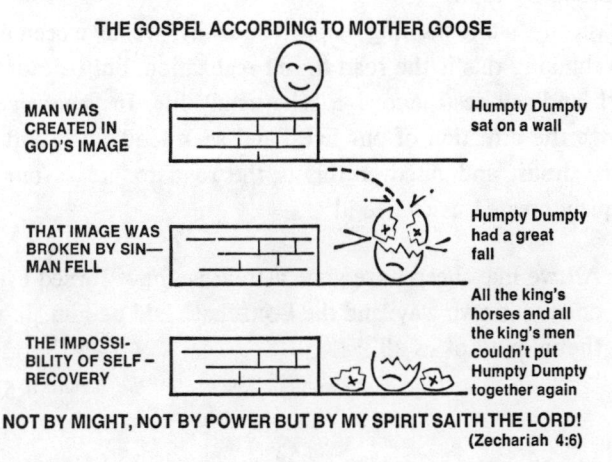

THE GOSPEL ACCORDING TO MOTHER GOOSE

MAN WAS CREATED IN GOD'S IMAGE — Humpty Dumpty sat on a wall

THAT IMAGE WAS BROKEN BY SIN— MAN FELL — Humpty Dumpty had a great fall

THE IMPOSSIBILITY OF SELF-RECOVERY — All the king's horses and all the king's men couldn't put Humpty Dumpty together again

NOT BY MIGHT, NOT BY POWER BUT BY MY SPIRIT SAITH THE LORD!
(Zechariah 4:6)

Humpty Dumpty was not a creature of his own making, nor was the wall upon which he sat. He had been placed there by another in a position of prominence and promise. Losing his heavenly orientation, he was tempted to lean over and look downward; to his dismay he discovered he had come under the power of gravity's earthly pull. Poor Humpty Dumpty had a horrible, shattering fall which left him broken—inside and out—in a totally irreparable way. Neither the wit, wisdom, or genius of the king's men nor the strength and power of the king's horses could put him back together again—ever!

Fortunately, unlike poor Humpty Dumpty, man has a Maker who in spite of *his* fall loved him enough to be willing to pay the price for his restoration. It cost Him the life of His Son, for it is only through His sacrificial death upon the cross as our Redeemer-Brother that we can find our way back into the family-purpose of our Heavenly Father. The power and doom of death was overcome by Jesus through a mighty Resurrection; the Holy Spirit Himself desires to impart that life to all who want to experience the redeeming love of God. Personal dignity and destiny can be restored to those who are willing to receive His grace and forgiveness in Christ Jesus, by confessing Him as their Lord and Saviour.

Basically, sin is wanting our will and way; we have been deceived into thinking this is the road to self-realization, but it leads only to death and self-destruction—a "shattered" life. In "conversion" we change the direction of our lives, and seek God's will and way in Christ Jesus, and discover this is the road to life as our Father uniquely created us to live it!

> All we like sheep have gone astray; we have turned every one to his own way; and the LORD hath laid on him [Jesus] the iniquity of us all.
>
> Isaiah 53:6

I [Jesus] am the way, the truth, and the life: no man cometh unto the Father, but by me.

John 14:6

For the wages of sin is death: but the gift of God is eternal life through Jesus Christ our Lord.

Romans 6:23

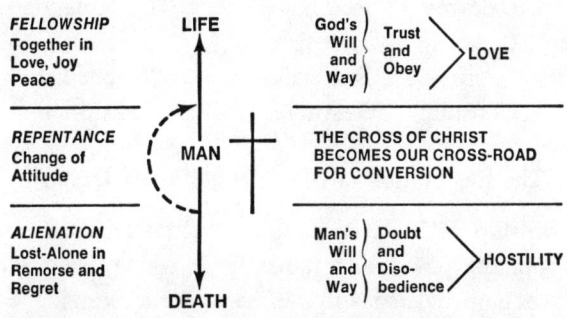

```
FELLOWSHIP          LIFE        God's  ⎫  Trust
Together in          ↑          Will   ⎬  and     ⎫ LOVE
Love, Joy                       and    ⎭  Obey    ⎭
Peace                           Way

─────────────────────────────────────────────────────
REPENTANCE                      THE CROSS OF CHRIST
Change of           MAN ──┼──   BECOMES OUR CROSS-ROAD
Attitude                        FOR CONVERSION
─────────────────────────────────────────────────────

ALIENATION                      Man's ⎫  Doubt
Lost-Alone in        ↓          Will  ⎬  and     ⎫ HOSTILITY
Remorse and                     and   ⎭  Diso-   ⎭
Regret            DEATH         Way      bedience
```

REPENTANCE = CHANGE OF HEART, MIND AND PURPOSE
CONVERSION = TO TURN AROUND — FROM / TOWARDS

Action—Reaction—Counteraction

God always initiates the action necessary for the fulfillment of His divine purpose. This was so in the creation of man. Satan then reacts in a fashion which was designed to frustrate God's original intention. This was so in the temptation and fall of man. Fortunately there are three acts to the drama of the ages, and the final scene displays the divine counteraction by which God's ultimate purpose is fulfilled. There may be many scenes involving the interplay between good and evil that intervene, but in the end, because of God's grace and sovereign power in Christ Jesus, we shall all find our identity in the Father's family and "live happily ever after"!

The following word study clearly establishes the principle involved, and becomes the basis for our personal redemption and restoration:

GOD ACTS	SATAN REACTS	GOD COUNTERACTS	CORRESPONDING NOUNS
Creates	Ruins	Redeems	Redemption
Constructs	Destroys	Restores	Restoration
Generates	Degenerates	Regenerates	Regeneration
Forms	Deforms	Reforms	Reformation
Covers	Uncovers	Recovers	Recovery
Conciliates	Alienates	Reconciles	Reconciliation
Institutes	Destitutes	Restitutes	Restitution

The Restoration of Man's Dignity and Destiny

The Lordship of Jesus is indeed the fountainhead from which streams both the power and the purpose which can produce the fulfillment of human personality. A fascinating account in the Gospels rather emphatically illustrates the principle involved. Jesus initiates what will develop into a rather dramatic discussion by asking the disciples a general and impersonal question: "Who do men say that I, the Son of man, am?" (*See* Matthew 16:13-26.)

Perhaps the disciples were flattered by the Lord's request. Usually they were the ones asking Him questions, but now He has turned to them for their evaluation of public opinion. They enthusiastically volunteer a variety of answers, all of which indicated that considerable confusion was in the minds of the people. There may have then followed a moment of silence as the disciples became uncomfortably aware that Jesus had not raised the question because He needed to be informed, but because He was preparing them for a second question which would be far more personal and specific: "But whom say ye that I am?"

Peter's ready response was both decisive and emphatic, "Thou art the Christ, the Son of the living God." I am sure the face of Jesus warmly displayed His pleasure and satisfaction, for He immediately commends Peter, using an interesting choice of words. "Blessed art thou, Simon Bar-jona [Simon, son of Jonah—born of an *earthly* father]: for flesh and blood [the mentality of man] hath not revealed it unto thee, but my Father which is in *heaven*" (modifications mine).

Peter had replied to Jesus' identity question by recognizing His *divine* Sonship and confessing that He was the Messiah—the Anointed One—who was to establish the Kingdom of God. It was a strong personal confession concerning the Lordship of Jesus Christ. The Lord's response is intriguing because it involves some interesting parallels:

1. Peter had recognized Christ's *divine* Sonship. In His reply Jesus recognizes Peter's *earthly* sonship, but also confesses that his revelation had been received from their *heavenly* Father.

2. Peter had under inspiration just confessed who Jesus was, and thereby personally established *His* identity. Now as if in like response, the Lord also confesses who Peter is and thereby establishes *his* identity. As Peter recognizes in Christ the "I AM" of God, so the Lord recognizes in Peter his little "I am" as it was to be realized in divine purpose.

"And I say also unto thee that *thou art* Peter [*petros*—masculine, a rocky fragment] and upon this rock [*petra*—feminine, a massive rock] will I build my church; and the gates of hell shall not prevail against it" (modifications mine).

Various church traditions have interpreted this passage in different ways. Some see the foundational rock as Peter himself; others feel it refers to Peter's revelation or his confession; while still another group believes it relates to the Person of the Lord Jesus. Perhaps the real answer involves a synthesis of truth from each of the various viewpoints, which should be seen as complementing rather than contradicting each other!

It would appear the Lord was informing Peter that he personally was to be a unique and significant part of a magnificent whole—the Church of Jesus Christ. While it is true that the Church's one foundation is Jesus Christ her Lord, that foundation also includes the apostles and the prophets who are essential and primary members of His Body. With Christ as the chief cornerstone, they form the foundation upon which a glorious temple of many "living stones" is to be erected. Each stone finds its purpose and "identity" only in relationship with all the other stones.

> For no man can lay a foundation other than the one which is laid, which is Jesus Christ.
>
> 1 Corinthians 3:11 NAS

> What a foundation you stand on now: the apostles and the prophets; and the cornerstone of the building is Jesus Christ himself! We who believe are carefully joined together with Christ as parts of a beautiful, constantly growing temple for God. And you also are joined with him and with each other by the Spirit, and are part of this dwelling place of God.
>
> Ephesians 2:20–22 LB

> And now you have become living building-stones for God's use in building his house. What's more, you are his holy priests; so come to him—[you who are acceptable to him because of Jesus Christ]—and offer to God those things that please him. As the Scriptures express it, "See, I am sending Christ to be the carefully chosen, precious Cornerstone of my church, and I will never disappoint those who trust in him." Yes, he is very precious to you who believe; and to those who reject him, well—"The same Stone that was rejected by the builders has become the Cornerstone, the most honored and important part of the building."
>
> 1 Peter 2:5–7 LB

A SIGNIFICANT PART OF A MAGNIFICENT WHOLE

Labels: The Body of Christ; Peter: a Model Man of God; Others: Men of Like Vision and Faith

THE CHURCH OF JESUS CHRIST

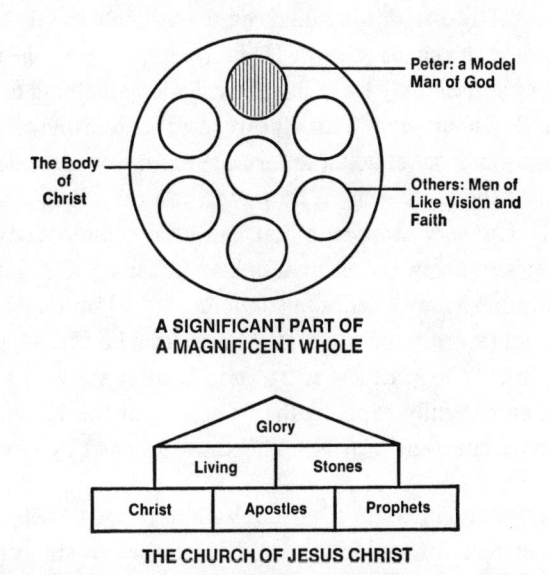

Glory — Living Stones — Christ | Apostles | Prophets

Peter was being prepared as a foundation stone to become the first of many gifted ministries which would form the solid basis for the early New Testament Church. These ministries would be expressed through the lives of men who like Peter were people of vision, faith, confession, and committment. Peter had been given a commission because of his confession. With that commission came his unique identity as a person. Peter had a purpose in life which conferred a dignity to his personality. The purpose for his life was to involve a responsible relationship to God's people. Apart from them he would lose his identity as a purpose-filled person, just as a building stone loses its reason for being when isolated from the structure for which it had been intended.

Self-surrender: The Key to Self-Realization

Jesus then proceeded to inform His disciples that His mission as the Messiah could be achieved only by way of the cross. The personal fulfillment of His own destiny involved the ultimate in self-surrender —His death at the hands of those He had come to save. The idea that one can find himself only by losing himself was something far beyond Peter's earthly mentality. With a heart filled with dismay Peter tries to argue the Lord out of going to Jerusalem. "At any cost, Jesus, you must by-pass the cross—that is no way to become a king . . . or build a church!" The very same man that had been commended by Jesus for his confession, now is censored for his confusion. "Get thee behind me, Satan: thou art an offence [a stumbling stone] unto me: for thou savourest not [are not mindful of] the things that be of God, but those that be of men"   (Matthew 16:23, modification mine).

Jesus then carefully explains the principles of the Kingdom concerning the attainment of true selfhood as designed by God.

> If any man will come after me, let him deny himself, and take up his cross, and follow me. For whosoever will lose his life for my sake shall find it. For what is a man profited if he shall gain the whole world and lose his own soul [true self]?
>
> Matthew 16:24–26

Peter had failed to see the difference between denial of "self" and the denial of "selfhood." Our selfhood has been uniquely created by God to reproduce and personally express the life of Jesus—our Model Brother. God never intended that personality should be destroyed or eliminated, as is the thesis of many oriental religions. Rather it is to reach its ultimate in perfection and expression—for we have been created in the very image of God.

The way to perfection, however, involves the principle of "self-denial." Otherwise we become self-centered, self-directed, and self-motivated. (The very same sickness that brought the downfall of Satan.) Divine destiny reaches heights far beyond the lifting power of self-realization. Water never rises beyond its source, and in like fashion it is totally impossible to lift oneself by oneself, beyond oneself! These principles can be outlined as follows:

REALIZATION OF SELFHOOD

A. NOT by self-realization:
1. Know yourself
2. Accept yourself   BY YOURSELF
3. Express yourself

B. NOT by self-elimination:
1. Depreciate yourself
2. Humiliate yourself   BY YOURSELF
3. Destroy yourself

C. BUT by self-surrender
1. Submit yourself
2. Yield yourself   TO JESUS CHRIST
3. Commit yourself

The true realization of selfhood involves submitting and committing ourselves to the very One into whose image we have been destined to be conformed. There is no greater goal. As we lose ourselves in Jesus Christ, we shall find ourselves living the abundant life which we were originally created to live. To lose ourselves in Him means to find our function as a member of the Body of Christ. It means taking our place among our brothers and sisters in the family of God. As "living stones" we are to fit together within the Church of Jesus Christ.

This involves the principle of submitting ourselves to one another in the bonds of Christ's love and through the power of the Holy Spirit. As we seek to recognize and realize divine destiny and dignity in others, we shall discover our own true selfhood. As I discover your identity and seek to know and promote your place and function in the family of God, I will at the same time be establishing my own identity. We need each other to become each other. The potential of personality can be realized only through relationship. I cannot be or function as a husband apart from my wife. I cannot be or function as a father apart from my children. I cannot be or function as a brother apart from my brothers and sisters in the family of God.

Jesus said, "Greater love hath no man than this, that a man lay down his life for his friends" (John 15:13). He also said, "Inasmuch as ye have done it unto one of the least of these my brethren, ye have done it unto me" (Matthew 25:40). Our lives are composed of our abilities, time, energy, desires, and possessions. To lay down our lives becomes very practical and personal in its expression. While it doesn't mean we submit to every demand someone places upon our lives for his own intentions, it does mean we submit to every demand the gracious Holy Spirit would place upon our lives that another might see, hear, feel, and thereby know the love of God—through us. It is in this kind of giving that we truly find ourselves in return. Any other attitude becomes a sieve through which our lives are quickly drained!

A Lesson From the Life of Peter

If we do not deny ourselves, we will deny the Lord and thereby lose our divine purpose for living. Peter learned this lesson by his triple denial of Jesus just prior to His Crucifixion (Matthew 26:69–75). In an endeavor to save and protect himself, he denied the very One who lovingly had invested His earthly life with the dignity of a heavenly commission. The life Peter wanted to save was now being sifted away by Satan himself (Luke 22:31). The sound of the crowing cock pierced through the cold night air straight into Peter's heart. An awful emptiness swept over his soul, for in denying the Lord he was in reality denying his own destiny. The future was void of meaning—there was nothing left to live for, and death held only the promise of an eternity of regret and remorse. (I recall once as a youth being overwhelmed with the chilling thought that I had crossed God's line of grace, and would be forever lost from His love. To think one must die and then face eternity without the Lord produces what can only be described as an "awful empty" feeling.)

Apart from God's great grace and Peter's wholehearted repentance, his life might have ended as tragically as did that of Judas. Both denied and betrayed the Lord in one sense. The difference lay in the basic condition of their hearts. Peter's failure was produced by a particular weakness in character which was exploited by Satan during a time of pressure. Basically he was committed to Jesus, or he would never have repented when confronted with the horrible reality of his sin. (It was Peter who once asked Jesus if forgiveness had a limit—Matthew 18:21.)

Judas's failure was the consummation of a deliberate and progressive hardening of his heart towards the love of Jesus. Basically, he was not committed to the Lord, for a self-serving attitude gradually developed which eventually infected his entire character. Jesus had warned the disciples that it was impossible to serve two masters at the same time. Judas had made his final choice in life, and by centering himself in himself, he lost what he sought to gain—his own soul (selfhood) —what a tragic conclusion, indeed, for a life that had in time held such great promise.

Peter's story, however, has a happy ending. By reaffirming his love-committment to Jesus, he is again commissioned to exercise Kingdom power by establishing and leading God's people with a shepherd's heart of love (John 21:15–19)—a love that will risk its life for the flock. Little did Peter know how very soon his role as a shepherd was going to be fulfilled in establishing the Church of Jesus Christ.

It happened on the day of Pentecost! Filled with and controlled by the Holy Spirit, Peter walks out upon a sea of hostile humanity and, without thought for his own life, boldly confesses the Lordship of Jesus Christ. The very gates of hell are shaken and give way as the prevailing power of Christ's Kingdom lays the foundation upon which the Church is to rest. A lot of "living stones" were brought together that day, and the process of mutual submission in the Holy Spirit began to produce the men and the ministries which would bring life to the Body of Jesus Christ.

Identity: Developed and Preserved Through Community

The Book of Acts is warm and personal in character. The record refers by name to almost fifty individuals whose lives were intimately involved in establishing and supporting the early Christian Church. A host of others are included indirectly. It is apparent that personal relationships within the life of the first Christian community were especially important. It was a loving, faithful, family fellowship in which individual members felt loved, wanted, respected, and secure. There were difficulties and sometimes disagreements, but ultimately the outcome was the development of Christian character in the life of each individual.

They indeed were being trained and prepared for a future which held many surprises. Probably most of them felt they would be a part of their local Christian community until Jesus returned again—an event they held to be imminent. Such was not the case, for unexpected persecution at the hands of Saul and others scattered them abroad "throughout the regions of Judea and Samaria" (Acts 8:1–4). Instead of extinguishing the flames of faith, the dispersion kindled new fires of community life all about the area.

One is reminded of the early efforts of men in the oyster industry who were trying to reduce the losses which they suffered through the predatory action of starfish in their oyster beds. They would drag the beds with nets in an endeavor to bring the starfish into their boats, where they promptly cut them into little pieces in order to destroy them. Unfortunately they then threw the remains overboard, not realizing that starfish have amazing powers of regeneration. Instead of reducing the starfish population, they multiplied their numbers many times over!

Such was the case in the early history of the Church. The severe winds of persecution merely scattered the sparks and fanned into flame new centers of community life. Undoubtedly each new community had as its basis a nucleus of members who were derived from the mother community in Jerusalem. Here was a core of people who were aware of their identity and ministry in the family of God. They supported one another that the results of evangelism could be conserved and integrated into the strength, wisdom, and security of the Christian community.

There is an interesting parallel from the world of nature. The structure of a simple sponge is fascinating to study. An outer wall surrounds an inner chamber which has a single outlet at the top. Small cylindrical cells shaped like napkin rings act as pores through which food-laden water can pass from the outside to the inner chambers. Outer epidermal cells are designed to provide a protective covering. Cells lining the inner chamber possess little funnel-shaped protoplasmic collars, which surround a single, whiplike flagellum. When all of the little "collar cells" are vigorously beating their flagella, sea water is drawn through the pore cells into the inner chamber and then forced out the topside excurrent opening. Nutrient particles and dissolved minerals in the sea water are trapped and ingested by the "collar cells." This is the only source of all the raw material that eventually is incorporated into the structure of the sponge.

Between the inner and outer layers of cells is a jellylike matrix in which are located a variety of specialized cells. Creeping ameboid cells transfer nutrients and raw materials ingested by the "collar cells" to surrounding cells to be used as fuel and building substance. Other cells form calcified or silicon spicules. Reproductive cells are also generated in this layer. The simple stationary sponge, therefore, is actually a highly developed little dynamo daily pumping many gallons of life-sustaining water through its structure. Here is a beautiful example of a cellular community in which each cell is identified by its function and contribution to the organism as a whole.

There is another amazing feature concerning the life-perpetuating powers of the lowly sponge. The organization of the sponge's cellular components can be totally disrupted by forcing them through a piece of cheesecloth. Isolated cells are thus formed. When left to themselves in a container of sea water a most remarkable phenomenon occurs. The various cells begin to aggregate together in little clumps. The epidermal cells migrate toward the outside of the clump while the "collar cells" move toward the center. The other cells in like fashion find their respective places, and many miniature sponges are thus formed, each with the potential of developing into a fully functioning organism!

As was true in the first Christian community, little may we realize how our present life situation may change in the future. One thing however, is certain: if we find our place and identity in the Body of Christ now as it relates to our local Christian community, we will be able to relate to other brothers and sisters in Christ wherever and whenever the occasion may arise. Perhaps this is the reason the Holy Spirit is bringing to God's people a greater appreciation for vital personal fellowship around Christ, regardless of our respective traditions and backgrounds. We need to recognize and respect each other in the Lord—submitting to that Word and work which God would have for us through the diverse ministries He has placed in the Body of Christ worldwide.

Identity: Defined Through Diversity With Unity

It has been my privilege to travel widely and find fellowship with Christians from a diversity of religious, racial, and cultural backgrounds. Occasionally there has been unintentional misunderstanding or disagreement, but ultimately we discovered that our need and desire for unity around Jesus was greater than the differences which could have separated us. By recognizing each other, our respective identities were not compromised, but further defined. We better understood who we were and what we weren't. It was the basis for a fellowship in which we were all enriched. Furthermore, we discovered there is an attractive life-force in the Holy Spirit which enabled us to worship, work, and witness together in a manner which clearly identified Jesus Christ as our common Lord!

I first became personally acquainted with the Eastern Orthodox tradition some years ago while attending the Third Ecumenical Fellowship at the Pontifical University in Salamanca, Spain. A meaningful friendship was established with one of the priests, who subsequently came to California to visit relatives and Orthodox Church leaders. He spent a day in our home and spoke at Melodyland Christian Center in the evening. After the service we planned to visit Disneyland, which was nearby. It was the only time available, since he was leaving very early the next morning. To our dismay we discovered the park had been privately engaged for the evening by the Shriners, and the gates had been closed to the general public.

We walked past the brightly colored entranceway and paused in the shadows of the parking area nearby. A policeman approached and inquired if he might be of some assistance. (I suppose we were rather obvious, since my priest friend was wearing his clerical garb.) We explained our situation and an interesting discussion developed. I began to feel that the hand of God was in our meeting under these unusual circumstances, and sought some opportunity to share the love of Jesus with our inquiring friend.

I mentioned that my visitor was an Eastern Orthodox priest and had that evening given his life story at Melodyland Christian Center just across the street. There was no response.

I continued by sharing that Father R. had been born in Russia, became involved with youth work in Yugoslavia and had been imprisoned for his active Christian witness. There was no response.

I then indicated that currently he was engaged by the British Broadcasting Company in beaming religious programs behind the Iron Curtain. Still no response!

The policeman then stated he wanted to make a phone call on our behalf, just in case there was a remote possibility he could get us in. After he left, I told Father R. that I felt the Lord had arranged our meeting, and he sensed the touch of God upon the affair as well. Upon the policeman's return, we were informed there was no way we could enter without rather obviously being recognized as "outsiders"! Our cordial conversation resumed, and I recall wishing something might be said that would clearly suggest to our friend that our meeting was more than just coincidence. We inquired concerning his family, and in response his life story followed. He was married and he and his wife were expecting their first child. His police work was for support while he pursued his Ph.D. program in mathematics. He had been in most of the European countries mentioned in our earlier discussion, and had at one time even studied for the priesthood in France.

He then made an interesting comment: "You will never guess who I met in Japan last summer—it was Oral Roberts—he was filming a television program! I have been in correspondance with him since then." I replied that I knew Oral Roberts personally and had previously chaired the Division of Natural Science at Oral Roberts University. As matters of mutual interest and concern developed, it became obvious to us all that our meeting was not by accident. I suggested Father R. might wish to pray that God's love and blessing would continue to grace the life of our brother and his family. He readily responded in a most gracious way.

I am sure it must have been an unusual sight to see. A policeman with his hat over his heart, a long-bearded, gray-robed Orthodox priest, and a baldheaded biology professor holding a prayer meeting in the front of Disneyland! As Father R. and I talked about it afterwards it dawned on us what God had done. He had taken two men who by culture, tradition, and background were certainly an example in contrast, and by His Spirit had united us in our prayer, worship, work, and witness that evening. In the process we had become better acquainted with each other and ourselves. Through mutual submission and respect in the Lord we had attained a level of life in the Spirit which allowed us to become an avenue of witness and blessing to a young policeman that God wished to uniquely reach in a most personal way. Only God could have arranged such an affair;

but what a meaningful lesson we learned about our brotherhood in Christ!

Concluding Challenge

In conclusion, may we listen again carefully to the wistful yet challenging words of our wise and wonderful Lord:

> "Whom do men say that I the Son of Man am?" . . .
> "Who do *you* say that I am?"

Gathered into that answer is our personal destiny for time and eternity. May we with Peter confess His Lordship, receive His commission, and fulfill our function in the family of God.

Come, let us deny ourselves, take up our cross daily and follow Jesus—for He alone is:

> The WAY to self-discovery,
> The TRUTH concerning self-surrender,
> Our LIFE as we were predestined to live it!

4
The When of Life

There is a rhythm to life which is as faithful in its expression as are the cycling stars in their orbits. Like a fine timepiece with its many little wheels and gears machined for precision in movement, so the machinery of life has been marvelously made and exquisitely adjusted for a perpetual performance. Life was never designed to extinguish itself in a miserable or offensive manner. There will be no rotten apples in heaven!

Even though man's original sin brought a curse upon the whole earthly realm, and there are many evidences of disorder, disease, discord, and ultimately death, still there is much of the original beauty, harmony, and divine balance which characterized the original Creation. We find a tenacity and tendency for life to continually and completely express itself. Life wants to live fully and forever!

Biological life has outwitted the designs of death by bridging from one generation to the next by the process of reproduction. This rhythmic repetition of birth, development, maturity, death, and decay is described in the life cycle of all living creatures. Relentlessly the wheels of life have rotated over the millenniums even though the earthly paths on which they move have drastically changed in character many times. Some forms have not been successful in coping with such changes and have become extinct, but others possessed the potential to adapt and have carried the torch of life faithfully to our present day.

Among those creatures who have been successful in the obstacle race of life has been man himself. Over the years the hand of the

Creator-Redeemer has carefully guarded the physical side of his makeup, for this is the "ground" from which life with a spiritual quality is to be eternally expressed. Jesus Christ is our pattern and guarantee. There is indeed a Man in the heavens; not a corpse, nor a ghost, but a man of flesh and bone—"glorified," but a real man!

An Eternal Heart's Desire

Eternal purpose is born into the heart of man and we are left with a feeling of frustration and futility if it is denied in our daily affairs. A sense of divine destiny brings our future into focus, and enables us to chart the direction of our lives with eternity in full view. Otherwise we become as ships at sea without a compass. We are tossed to and fro by the wind and the waves, but have no home port towards which we are headed. Each day becomes an end in itself, and the direction of our lives moves in ceaseless circles. In frustration we may churn the waters into a white froth, as if much motion will make up for our lack of purpose. Or, some in resignation may idle away the time in ever widening circles of days and months and years, not really knowing where they have been—or where they are going.

A young college student wrote to me once and confessed that, to her, life was just a relentless round of meaninglessness. She concluded each day with an awareness that the next would be as empty as was the last. Several times I have heard people say that their whole life had been a total waste! They were echoing the conclusion to which the writer of Ecclesiastes came after endeavoring to fill the eternal void in his life with temporal pleasures, pursuits, and purposes (*see* Ecclesiastes, chapter 2). These are his words:

> In my opinion, nothing is worthwhile; everything is futile. For what does a man get for all his hard work? Generations come and go but it makes no difference. The sun rises and sets and hurries around to rise again. The wind blows south and north, here and there, twisting back and forth, getting

nowhere. The rivers run into the sea but the sea is never full, and the water returns again to the rivers, and flows again to the sea.
Ecclesiastes 1:2–7 LB

He then reviews the many rhythms expressed in life:

To every thing there is a season, and a time for every matter or purpose under heaven: A time to be born and a time to die; a time to plant, and a time to pluck up what is planted. A time to kill, and a time to heal; a time to break down, and a time to build up . . .
Ecclesiastes 3:1–3 AMPLIFIED

The beauty and purpose of the orderly (timely) life is only discovered, however, as it is related to God's eternal plan for man's existence —a plan which man cannot comprehend apart from divine revelation:

He has made everything beautiful in its time; He also has planted eternity in men's heart and mind (a divinely implanted sense of a purpose working through the ages which nothing under the sun, but only God, can satisfy), yet so that man cannot find out what God has done from the beginning to the end.
Ecclesiastes 3:11 AMPLIFIED

As discussed in an earlier chapter, the God of eternity graciously broke through the time barrier when in Jesus He revealed His everlasting love and purpose for us as His people. There is therefore both success and fulfillment in coordinating our life with His.

Biological success is determined by the extent to which the potential of natural life is realized in time, place, and character. In other words, a species would be considered successful if it occupies every niche (suitable habitat) available, fully expresses its unique form and function, and extends itself in time through the rhythm of reproduction.

There are some obvious and interesting parallels when the above criteria are applied to success as it relates to our life in the Spirit. As we have discussed previously, the eternal desire of our Heavenly Father is that the lovely life of His Son may be extended through a family of many sons who forever would uniquely display the noble nature of their Elder Brother. Forever begins now, and God's glorious purpose includes our world, for it was here that man was created and given the commission to fill the whole earth with life!

Rhythms of Life

One of the most fascinating life cycles to study in the animal world is that of the grunion. These are small, silvery fish which breed from March through July along the coast of Southern California. They lay their eggs in the sand, and an incubation period of two weeks is necessary before they are ready to hatch. What is so intriguing about the entire process is the precise timing which is necessary if the little fish are to be successful. They can deposit their eggs only on the third or fourth night after a new or full moon. Furthermore, this must be accomplished during a crucial 15-minute period following the peak night tide. The critical nature of the timing is related to the height of the tides. The eggs must be buried, incubated and hatched in rhythm with the sea. The peak biweekly high tide is necessary or the eggs would be washed away by subsequent tides before incubation was complete, and the little fish embryos would be destroyed. Fortunately they are ready to hatch just as the next peak tide occurs two weeks later. The little eggs burst like popcorn, releasing millions of baby fish into the receding waves of the waiting sea, and the wheel of life has turned once more!

Of course there are many other cycles in nature with which we are familiar. The "circadian" (*circa*—about; *dies*—day) or daily rhythms of life are perhaps the most common. With each revolution of the earth there are corresponding changes in such environmental factors as light and temperature. Various neurological and biochemical mechanisms are affected, and patterns of eating, resting, and activity are thereby controlled. Internal biological clocks are set and run according to rather precise rhythms. All we have to do to appreciate their significance is get out of time with our interior clockwork and see what happens. After a jet plane trip through several time zones it usually requires several days to reset the timing of our physical functions.

Just as there are seasons, cycles, and rhythms which are crucial to life in the natural, so is there a divine timing to life in the realm of the Spirit.

One of the ways in which our Enemy seeks to limit the Lord's will for our lives is by inducing us to break step with God's timing. This may occur indirectly through soulish or carnal tendencies in our lives which need the discipline of the Holy Spirit. Occasionally it may be by direct satanic impulse. In either case we are tempted to leap ahead or lag behind the schedule God has planned for us.

A "hasty spirit" is characterized by an impatient, impulsive, and presumptuous personality pattern. The very first temptation which man faced may well have included an appeal to shortcut one's way to personal fulfillment. Could it have been that the fruit of the Tree of Knowledge (death) was ripe and ready to be eaten, while the fruit of the Tree of Life required time for it to reach its season of maturity? (See Psalms 1:3.)

Jesus was likewise tempted by Satan in the wilderness to prematurely break His fast by turning stones into bread. It was not the devil's prerogative, however, to determine when or how the temptation period was to be concluded. Jesus waited upon the will of His Father in loving obedience in regard to His natural needs and desires. As a result He received the personal ministry of the holy angels (Matthew 4:1–11). "Angel food" is worth waiting for!

Satan's suggestion that Jesus dramatically leap from the temple pinnacle to the crowded arena below was calculated to rush Him into an earthly kingdom, at the same time forestalling the coming of God's heavenly Kingdom, which always awaits a spiritual preparation in the hearts of men. How easily He could have missed that for which, in His humanity, He had waited some thirty years. A single move made in presumption and haste would have spoiled what had been cherished in the heart of the Father since before the foundation of the world!

Yes, Jesus is our Model Brother, who perfectly sets the pattern which we are to follow—always in time and in step with the will of our Heavenly Father.

Sequenced and Synchronized

After my wife and I had discovered the beautiful reality of the Spirit-filled life, we had a deep desire to share our new-found joy with others, little realizing where that desire would eventually take us the world over. At the time, however, I was teaching biology in a small college in the Midwest and longed to be more actively involved in the vision God had given us concerning a fresh move of His Holy Spirit which eventually would reach into the very heart of the historic churches themselves.

For many months I encouraged the Lord to quicken His pace, for certainly He didn't want to waste His time or mine! (I have found that approach is not particularly impressive to Someone who has made the ages of time in the first place.) The only answer I seemed to receive was that God's will and purpose for me was to learn to wait upon Him in love and obedience.

When the time came for us to move to a Christian college on the West Coast it was with peace and a certainty that we were in God's will. It was another two years, however, before the Holy Spirit broke forth in keeping with our earlier vision. By that time God had brought everything to a place of preparation which only then became apparent. The process involved several principles which are worth considering. The development and perfection of God's purpose in our lives has many parallels with the developmental process as studied in embryology.

The development of a little fertilized egg into the complex organism characteristic of its species involves many different stages and steps. There is a sequence or order in time to the various phases of development. Furthermore, at any given time the separate parts and processes must be synchronized in their activity. No process is occuring in an isolated fashion, but in concert with many other processes. In a musical composition not only must the right chords follow one another in a prescribed sequence, but at every point in time all of the individual notes which produce a chord must be perfectly harmonized. Sequence (order) and synchronization (coordination) are the key words.

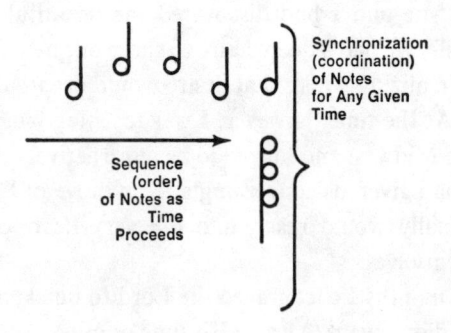

In the development of the lens of the eye the two ideas are beautifully illustrated. A stalklike extension of the embryonic midbrain grows towards the nearby epidermis (skin) of the head region. The end of the stalk expands and indents to form a cuplike structure. As it approaches the overlying epidermis, the stalk becomes the optic nerve, while the eyecup itself will develop into the inner layers and retina of the adult eye. It will also chemically induce the epidermis to thicken, protrude inwardly, and eventually pinch off to form the lens of the eye, which is now situated in the open end of the eyecup.

Experimental studies on amphibians have shown that an eyecup transplanted under the epidermis of either older or younger embryos cannot induce lens formation, because the epidermis is responsive only at a particular time in the developmental process. However, if an eyecup is transplated at the right time, but to an abnormal site—such as epidermis covering the belly—it will induce the formation of a lens, and ultimately an entire eye will form. It is obvious that in the complex of developmental events the right parts and processes have to be in the right places at the right time, performing their proper functions. One miscue in the early stages of development can profoundly affect the outcome of the entire process. It is a wonder we are as normal as we are. Truly, embryonic development is one of the most marvelous miracles associated with life!

The development of God's will in our lives often involves a complexity far beyond our understanding. People, places, events all are in the process of being sequenced and coordinated, yet without violating the freedom in man with which he has been endowed. God patiently and persistently works His will through the maze of human affairs in a most marvelous way. He begins with us as individuals and carefully shapes us as we yield ourselves to His ultimate purpose. In the process He often allows us to walk in limited light, for a limited time, for a limited purpose. Once the purpose has been fulfilled we are ready to move on, often in a different direction.

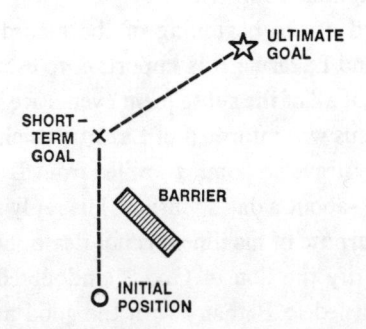

Sometimes barriers of ignorance, prejudice, immaturity, or circumstances prevent us from seeing God's ultimate goal. He therefore allows us a short-term goal in another direction which we can see. In obtaining this immediate goal, we are brought beyond our barrier and now can redirect our course towards His ultimate purpose. Since the process involves an ongoing sequence of events, we must maintain our dependency upon the guidance of the Holy Spirit.

In retrospect, God's guidance in our lives closely paralleled many of the principles just discussed. Upon arriving on the West Coast we realized that God's purpose for spiritual renewal went far beyond anything we could have imagined and involved the coordination of many other lives and situations. Some of the spiritual lessons we were to learn from others hadn't yet been accomplished in their own experience! Fortunately, God had wisely ignored all of my passionate pleas to "get the show on the road," and had graciously sequenced all of the preparatory phases with divine precision for all involved.

Divine Delays for Divine Purpose

I have discovered that divine delays are timed for divine purpose. Not one minute is wasted, contrary to our way of thinking, if we are waiting in faith and obedience upon God. There are many illustrations of divine delays in Scripture which persuasively point out the principle. Perhaps one of the most familiar is contained in the account of Lazarus's resurrection (John 11).

We are advised at the beginning of the record that Jesus *loved* Martha, Mary, and Lazarus. It is important to establish the fact, for that assures us that all of the subsequent events are within the context of God's love. Jesus was informed of Lazarus's sickness by a messenger who probably traveled some 20 miles from Bethany into Perea, where Jesus was—about a day's journey. His reply is one of hope and comfort: "The purpose of his illness is not death, but for the glory of God; it is to glorify the Son of God." Undoubtedly the messenger immediately returned to Bethany with the good news, not knowing that Lazarus had already died shortly after his departure. Nevertheless, the sisters may have been encouraged—for had not the Master raised the daughter of Jairus (Matthew 9:22–26) and the widow's son at Nain (Luke 7:11–17)? Furthermore, according to popular tradition among the Jews the soul hovered over the body for three days before its final departure, giving hope for a possible resuscitation.

In light of the urgency of the situation the Lord's response is somewhat puzzling to the natural mind, for we are informed that Jesus remained where He was for two more days. By now Lazarus has been buried for three days, and the traditional seven-day mourning period was well under way in Bethany. The disciples were unaware of what had transpired, but Jesus knew. For two days He carried alone His concern for Mary and Martha—with great feeling and heaviness of heart. I think we have failed to appreciate how difficult it was for Jesus to restrain Himself from immediately going to the side of those whom He loved so deeply. I am sure the night was spent in earnest prayer and communion with His Heavenly Father.

After the two-day interval, the Lord was released in His Spirit concerning the trip to Bethany and announced His intention to return to Judea. The disciples were alarmed, for the Jews were seeking to take His life. Jesus responded by assuring them they would be walking in the light and safety of God's will—they were in step and on time!

The Lord then informed them of the death of Lazarus and added the rather strange words, "I am glad for your sakes that I was not there." His gladness was not because Jesus was without feeling for those involved—for He was deeply disturbed—but because, through the tragedy, the joy and glory of God's will would be revealed. The delay was filled with divine purpose!

It was on the fourth day after Lazarus's burial that Jesus and the disciples at last arrived at Bethany. By now the finality of his death had extinguished whatever hope may have remained—except perhaps for Martha. They had waited anxiously for the arrival of Jesus after the messenger's return. Surely He would come as quickly as possible, for wouldn't real love seek to spare those loved unnecessary pain and anguish? Hours of anxious grief turned into days of bewilderment, and finally despair. Then Jesus came!

Faith Leaps the Limitations of Time

Martha rushed to meet the Lord at the edge of town, and in the ensuing discussion the bright light of divine purpose began to break through the dark clouds of doubt and disappointment. "Martha, I myself am the resurrection and the life! Do you *believe* this?" Although perplexed, Martha's reply was strong and certain, "I do believe you are the Christ, the Son of God who was to come into the world." His presence and her confession strengthened her faith and brought renewed hope to her heart for whatever the Lord was about to do.

Immediately she informed Mary at His request that Jesus had finally arrived. Accompanied by the wailing mourners, Mary fell at Jesus' feet and, like Martha, exclaimed, "Lord, if only you had been here my brother would not have died!" Here again was an expression of faith, but qualified by the limitations of time—and time had run out! Jesus did not pause as with Martha to build her faith by His word; perhaps she was too grief-stricken to respond. (How wise and gentle Jesus was with Mary. Emotionally she was less stable—but perhaps more sensitive—than Martha. Jesus did not demand as much from her as He did her stronger sister, but supported her weakened faith with His love and understanding. The Lord was not so preoccupied with the making of a miracle that He could not personally relate to everyone involved.) Martha's faith had increased, however, and the disciples, though unsure of all that Jesus intended to do, had obediently and faithfully followed Him to Bethany at the risk of their lives. Even elementary faith will create a permissive atmosphere in which Jesus can minister!

This personal confrontation with death and its consequences upon those whom Jesus loved moved our Lord to tears. Death is the final outcome of sin's power over man, and Jesus responded with both intense anger and grief. I have tried to picture the face of Jesus as it was seen by those who were close enough to feel both His compassion for the bereaved and His holy indignation concerning Satan, sin, death, and the grave. I am sure an indelible impression was etched into the hearts and minds of the onlookers which would never fade from their memories. Furthermore, the faithless and hostile attitude of some of the mourners deeply distressed the Lord. By their loud cries they claimed to be sympathetic with the sorrowing sisters, but in no way were they prepared to endorse Jesus or His ministry—even if it should involve raising Lazarus from the dead!

Moving with determination and divine authority, Jesus decisively instructs them to remove the stone from the entrance of the tomb. This direct confrontation with death and its devastating power caused Martha to question the Lord's command. He gently but firmly reminded her that if she would believe she would see the glory of God.

The record then simply reads, "So they took away the stone"! I have wondered who the "they" were. I have a feeling only the disciples themselves would have dared to obey such an extraordinary command. Furthermore, they had personally been involved in the previous delay, and Jesus Himself had informed them that it was for a divine purpose—that God might be glorified, and through that glory their faith in His Son would be strengthened and sharpened. So without hesitation they rolled the stone aside and stood facing the mouth of the freshly opened grave with Mary, Martha, a mixed crowd of stunned and skeptical onlookers—and Jesus. The silent power of death's presence swept over the people like the still that follows the last whisper of life's breath. Then Jesus looked up to heaven and spoke: "Father, thank You for hearing me, as You always do, but I said it because of the people standing here that they will believe that You have sent me." Then He shouted, "Lazarus, come out!" And out Lazarus came —bound up in graveclothes. "Unbind him and let him go home," Jesus said. And so many of the Jews who had come with Mary and had seen what Jesus had done believed on Him; but some of them went to the Pharisees and told them what He had done ... so from that time on the Jewish leaders began plotting His death. (This account paraphrased from various versions of the Scriptures.)

As one rehearses the stirring story of Lazarus's resurrection, it is obviously filled with divine and glorious purpose for the lives of all involved. How little any of them could have imagined a few days earlier what soon was to transpire. It all happened so suddenly: Lazarus's illness, his unexpected death, the delayed return of Jesus—and then the resurrection! For Mary, Martha, and Lazarus a new and glorious relationship of faith and love for Jesus had been established. Furthermore, their relationships with each other reached a new level of love, loyalty, and appreciation. Tradition tells us Lazarus was about thirty when he first died and that he lived another thirty years thereafter. One can well imagine they were in the upper room on the day of Pentecost, and personally contributed to the formation of the first Christian community.

For the disciples, the experience was a preparation for the forthcoming death, burial, and Resurrection of their Lord. They were soon to see in a full and final way that Jesus was indeed the glorious Lord of both life and death, and herein was their personal guarantee of resurrection life!

The Jewish observers were given the glorious opportunity of acknowledging Jesus as the Christ—the Messiah Himself. Many did believe; but others refused to acknowledge Him as the Lord of their lives, and reported Him to the Pharisees, who immediately sought to bring about His demise.

For Jesus, the *resurrection* of Lazarus prepared the way for His *death!* It was the final turning point which headed our Lord to His cross and our redemption. Then following another divine delay of three days, resurrection power would triumph over sin, hell, death, and the grave—and God would indeed be glorified! (John 12:23-28).

Why Did God Wait So Long?

I shall never forget an experience which occurred after a meeting where I had spoken on the healing power of our Heavenly Father's love. Many had testified of deep hurts and scars which had been graciously healed as they responded to the loving-kindness and tender mercy of their Father God. One young lady remained behind, however, and through tear-filled eyes confessed that as a youth leader she knew in her head that God loved her, yet she was unable to feel it in her heart!

Her girlhood years and family relationships had been lovingly wholesome, and there seemed to be no reason from these areas for the present pain which I could feel had reached to the very center of her relationship with God. She was a beautiful girl, but her lovely features were marred by the hurt of a bewildered, bruised, and broken heart. Only after a time of gentle and compassionate counsel did the real reason for her distress come to the surface. She had only recently suffered a deep disappointment which in her eyes had brought the love of God into question.

She had surrendered her whole life to the Lord and wanted only His will in all of her earthly relationships. This had included a desire for God's best in regard to a life-companion with whom she could share the joy and beauty of a Christ-honoring home and family. Such a young man had indeed come into her life, and the future was filled with happy hope and holy expectation. Their wedding date had been set, and all of the joyful preparations which surround such a beautiful occasion were under way. Then it happened!

Her fiance had been a man with an apparently dual personality. A spirit of delusion had at some time entered his life, and the associated mental instability surfaced unexpectedly just prior to their forthcoming marriage. Consequently, he was committed to a mental institution, and in a matter of moments her future—so bright with promise—was filled with disappointment and despair. She had endeavored to steady herself in the Lord as best she could, but nagging doubts concerning God's love began to rise within her heart and cast disturbing shadows upon her whole relationship with the Lord. "All I wanted was God's will in every area of my life, Dr. Frost. Why did He wait so long before letting me know the true situation concerning my fiance? If my Heavenly Father really loved me, why did He delay?"

It is at such times that any counselor feels totally dependent upon the faithfulness of the Holy Spirit to inspire words of truth and love which can cleanse and heal the wounded heart and restore the soul to divine health again. The direction came from the little word "delay" which was the key hidden in the young lady's plea for help and healing.

I shared with her that when our lives are truly committed to Christ, there are no delays in our walk with Him that are not filled with divine purpose, even though at the time we may feel or see very little in the natural which makes sense at all. Together we considered several situations from Scripture, including that of Lazarus's resurrection, which established God's loving purpose in all things at all times. The Apostle Paul is obviously speaking from personal experience when he emphatically declares:

> For we know (absolutely) that *all* things work together for good to those who love God and are called according to His design and *purpose*. For from the very beginning God decided that those who come to Him—and all along He knew who would—*should become like His Son,* so His Son would be the First, with many brothers.
>
> Romans 8:28-29 (paraphrased)

The Lord never promised us that everything that happens to us will be good; but that He would work everything *together* for good—the goodness of Christ's character and life! We are not spared from all of the accidents and tragedies of life, but are assured of His redeeming presence. What He doesn't *protect* us from, He will *deliver* us out of, or *perfect* us through. I then shared with this lovely maiden of God that her Heavenly Father had not forgotten her, but desired that she accept His gracious comfort and consolation and also His assurance that He would make it up to her, here in time as well as in eternity. To her would be given the special privilege of ministering His healing love to many who like herself had experienced a tragedy in life. God would give her great compassion and understanding, which others would feel and thereby be encouraged in their approach to her for help.

Together we reviewed the beautiful and meaningful testimony from the life and pen of the Apostle Paul:

> We should like you, our brothers, to know something of what we went through in Asia. At that time we were completely overwhelmed; the burden was more than we could bear; in fact we told ourselves that this was the end. Yet we believe now that we had this experience of coming to the end of our tether that we might learn to trust, not in ourselves, but in God who can raise the dead.
>
> 2 Corinthians 1:8–9 PHILLIPS
>
> Thank God, the Father of our Lord Jesus Christ, that He is *our* Father and the source of all mercy and comfort. For He strengthens and comforts us in our afflictions and troubles that we in turn may be able to sympathetically share that consolation with others in their time of need.
>
> 2 Corinthians 1:3, 4 (paraphrased)

It was like watching a resurrection. The warm healing light of God's love brought new hope and life to the failing heart of one of God's dearest daughters. Yes, He loved her, and through that love a ministry of love was born that day—which graciously would last forever! Once again God had redeemed a time of waiting and wondering by relating it to eternal purpose and divine glory!

Rouse Your Reluctant Spirit

If our Enemy cannot tempt us to leap ahead of God by firing within us a "hasty spirit," he often moves to the other extreme and paralyzes us with a "reluctant spirit"—which causes us to lag behind. A "reluctant spirit" can be fed by a lazy, fearful, indecisive, or critical attitude towards life.

The Prophet Amos warned God's people of the danger of being "at ease in Zion" (Amos 6:1). This was an obvious reference to an attitude of complacent comfort and moral indifference. It would also include an element of spiritual laziness. They had been given the privilege of presenting to the pagan nations the law and love of God, which held the only promise for lasting peace and prosperity among the peoples of the earth.

It is easy to condemn Israel and Judah for their repeated failures in light of God's clear instructions concerning their divine privileges and responsibilities. In effect we imply the story would have been much different if we had been on the scene. Well, we weren't then, but we are now—and for such an hour as *this* have we come to the Kingdom!

I recall praying what I thought was a rather respectable prayer one morning while driving to the college where I was teaching. I fervently prayed that God would take the day and our lives and redeem the time for His glorious purpose in Christ Jesus. It really didn't sound like a half-bad prayer, and I was rather pleased my wife was with me to hear it. However, the Lord stopped me right in the middle, and abruptly informed me that He couldn't answer a prayer like that for it wasn't even scriptural. "It's not My responsibility to redeem the time, but *yours*—through the power of the Spirit!" (*See* Ephesians 5:14-18.)

To redeem the time, we must know what God is doing, where and how He's doing it, and through whom. We are then responsible for relating ourselves to His people as together, in His Spirit, we bring a witness of His love to our world. This involves some initiative on our part to investigate and actively become involved. God is sweeping across the face of the earth with the fresh breath of His Spirit in a renewal of true Christian fellowship and witness. Men and women of all traditions—and no tradition—are being flooded by God's Spirit and united in the common cause of sharing the life and love of Jesus with others in a warm, personal way. Worship becomes alive and is an expression of the heart, as once more the joy of the Lord becomes an abiding source of strength. How very much the Holy Spirit seeks to inspire us to be up and about our Father's business, for the hour is later than we think.

There never has been an hour such as this in all of history past. There is a unique quality and character to our age which has never been attained heretofore. With the current emphasis on the population and pollution explosions—coupled with the threat of resource exhaustion—we have the uneasy feeling that time might be running out. These problems have caused tensions and conflicts on an international scale.

There has been an explosion of knowledge as well. Only the advent of computers has permitted this increase in information to be efficiently stored and retrieved. Sadly, man's heart has not expanded in keeping with his head, and what hope there may have been for an "intellectual" solution to the evils of our world has quickly given way to despair. Advances in communication and transportation technology have shrunken our world to the point that any country is now but a stone's throw from another—but look at the kinds of stones we can throw! Never before in the history of mankind has man had in his hands the power to eliminate life from the face of the globe; in fact, we now talk in terms of "overkill potential"! The *Bulletin of the Atomic Scientists* was born during the advent of this nuclear age. It has over the years addressed itself to the critical character of our day and time. On the cover of each issue is the face of a clock, the hands of which are set for the midnight striking hour of doom. Just recently the minute hand was again moved forward—indicating there were but seven minutes left in the hourglass of time!

Magnitude or Quantity

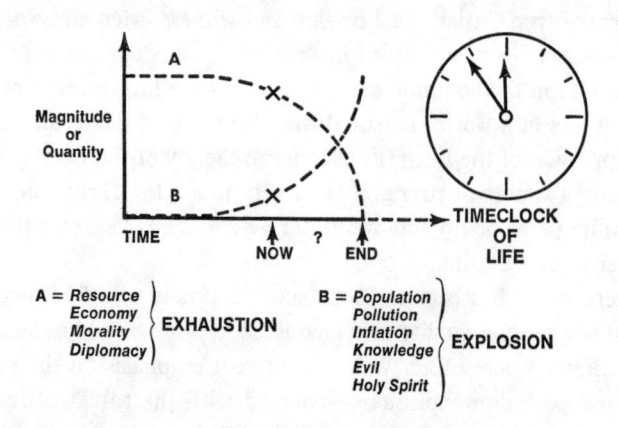

TIME — NOW — ? — END → TIMECLOCK OF LIFE

A = Resource, Economy, Morality, Diplomacy } EXHAUSTION

B = Population, Pollution, Inflation, Knowledge, Evil, Holy Spirit } EXPLOSION

In the light of our times the following passage from Scripture presents a powerful prophetic message:

> You know what a critical hour this is, how it is high time now for you to wake up out of your sleep—rouse to reality. For salvation (final deliverance) is nearer to us now than when we first believed. The night is far gone, the day is almost here. Let us then drop the deeds of darkness and put on the full armor of light, and live as children of the day; not in reveling, immorality, sensuality, quarreling, or jealousy. Rather clothe yourself with the Lord Jesus Christ and make no provision for the passions of your lower nature.
>
> Romans 13:11-14 (paraphrased)

While some might lag behind God's end-time will and purpose out of complacency, others fall back out of fear for the future. Yet Jesus said that when all of these things come to pass we are not to be "shook up" but to "look up, for your redemption draweth nigh" (Luke 21:28). Scriptures declare that in the last days there indeed will be an "explosion" of evil as the Enemy moves with great wrath, seeing he has but a short time left (Revelation 12:12). However, we are not left helpless and hopeless, for in the last days there is also to be a great outpouring of the Holy Spirit upon all flesh—a mighty countercurrent which shall unite God's people in love and bring forth a final witness to the world (Acts 2:17-21; Matthew 24:14).

Rather than being paralyzed with fear, we are to rise up in the strength of His joy, and in a responsible way redeem the time for His glorious end-time purpose, and thereby even hasten the day of His appearing (Nehemiah 8:10; 2 Peter 3:11, 12). Some of us who are ultraconservative in nature and wish to see every aspect of an issue and anticipate every possible turn of events, often miss the crucial time of decision in the process. This was my mentality at one time; I was so afraid of missing God's will that I lost my joy on the teeter-totter of uncertainty. Finally the Lord instructed me to take in faith every opportunity to share Jesus that came my way, unless He said no! It is much easier to hear the voice of the Lord when peace and faith fill the inner sanctuary of our souls. Otherwise, our doubts and fears so rattle around in our minds as we seesaw back and forth that the inner noise and confusion drown out the still, small voice of the Spirit. If we get our orders garbled, we may go marching off in the wrong direction, out of step, out of time, and unrelated to the fellowship in Christ's Body to which God has called us.

Our Divine Pacemaker

Inhibitory and accelerator nerves of the central nervous system regulate the rhythm of the heart by controlling a "pacemaker" center in the upper heart chambers (atria). The timing of the contractions of the lower chambers (ventricles) is regulated by a bundle of nerves that pass from the upper to lower chambers. In this way both the rhythm and phase of the contractions are synchronized. If the chambers were to beat independently—a condition known as "heart block" —the effective output would be greatly reduced. Occasionally another situation can arise in which the individual muscle fibers of the ventricles come out from under their corporate control and begin to twitch in an uncoordinated fashion, which prevents a forceful contraction of the chambers from occurring at all. The condition is called "fibrillation," and the cardiac output is reduced to zero—a situation obviously incompatible with the need for sustained circulation. Unless the heart can be electrically "shocked" back into a synchronized rhythm, death will follow immediately. The experience of seeing and feeling a fibrillating heart under experimental laboratory conditions makes an indelible impression.

It is so comforting to know that the Blessed Holy Spirit, as our "Divine Pacemaker," can adjust and retime our lives if we will personally yield ourselves to Him. He so wants to regulate our daily affairs and affections that our hearts begin to beat as one with His. The Lord is looking for those like David, of whom He can say, "There is 'a man after mine own heart'!" (See Acts 13:22.) It is also encouraging to see the way in which God's love is beginning to bring us together that there might be a coordinated expression of His life. Only the pulsating power of the Holy Spirit can corporately relate and regulate our lives that the Body of Christ will truly and fully express the life of her Lord. It is a glorious hour in which to live: indeed, this could be the generation which will herald the coming of our Lord Jesus Christ Himself. May we hasten the day of His appearing.

"Even so, come quickly, Lord Jesus!"

5
The Where of Life

Ecology is one of the most important and interesting of the biological sciences. Until the recent emphasis on the conservation of natural resources, the term was hardly known outside of the biological field; now it is almost a household word. The word "ecology" is derived from two Greek terms: *oikos* (house, dwelling place) and *logos* (science, study). Ecology, therefore, refers to the study of living things in relationship to their environment; in other words, it deals with the mutual involvement between life and its location. The character of the environment determines the kind of life which it will support; but once life is established, it has the power to change its environment!

The harsh barren surface of a rough and rugged rock hardly seems a suitable place for any living thing. Yet this is the preferred habitat for the hardy lichen, which is readily identified as a grayish-green incrustation that doesn't look very much alive at all—but it is! In fact, it has the power not only to weather the bitter winds of winter but also to withstand the withering rays of the summer sun.

Actually, the lowly lichen is not a solitary plant but two mutually interdependent organisms living in such a close, intimate relationship with each other that it takes a microscopic examination to distinguish their component parts. One partner in the relationship is a simple green algae which can photosynthesize organic nutrients, its color coming from the pigment chlorophyl, which has the peculiar ability to convert light energy into a useful form of chemical energy. It has little water-absorbing ability, however, and would quickly dry up if it were not for its close association with a friendly fungus. The spongy fungus does not possess chlorophyl pigment; therefore, it is totally dependent upon the green algae for its supply of organic nutrients. It does have the excellent quality of absorbing and conserving water!

Linked Together for Life

The two organisms literally link up together for life. Neither could live without the other; together, they not only exist, but actually become the ground which will support yet higher forms of life. Acid by-products of the living lichens attack the rock substrate to which they are attached. Tiny rock particles associated with the decomposing remains of lichens form a thin layer of soil in which little tufts of green moss now can grow. As the mossy cover thickens and increases in size along the length of rocky cracks and crevices, it becomes sufficiently rich and deep to support the root systems of ferns and flowering plants. Eventually even tree seedlings can set themselves in the soil thus prepared, and the silent life-power of their growing root systems have been known to split the rocks in which they grew. Such is the potential of the "little" lichen!

The Scripture informs us that we are not to "despise the day of small things"—for through such, God accomplishes His great and glorious purposes. The Lord is looking for those who will intimately link their lives with His, and thereby be lifted beyond their own limitations. God is building His Church, but He has chosen to accomplish His purpose with and through His people. Apart from God we *cannot* construct His living Church; but apart from us, He *will not* —for He has sovereignly committed Himself to working with and through us as co-laborers! (Mark 16:20; 1 Corinthians 3:5-16). Paradise will ultimately be regained on the very same ground upon which it was lost—on earth, through man. The Son of man, through His redemptive victory upon the cross, reclaimed the "title-deed" from the god of this world, that the sons of men might occupy and reign with Him upon an earth recovered and restored!

You recall it was the intimate life relationship between the members of the little lichen that enabled it to overcome the adverse elements, and ultimately recover the sterile surface of a ravished rock. In like fashion God desires that our lives be so closely related to His Son, through the unifying power of His Spirit, that we may accept our divine responsibility for the recovery and restoration of a Creation cursed by sin, but reclaimed by our Saviour. Christ was afflicted that the whole world might be healed. As we share together in His life, we become ministers of His healing power to all aspects of Creation, which has been crippled by Satan through man's rebellion and sin. Resurrection power holds the promise and is the provision for the divine recovery of all things. God's will shall yet be done on earth as it is in heaven!

The Scriptures emphatically support our expectations concerning our "so great" salvation:

> Dear Brothers, I realize that what you did to Jesus was done in ignorance, as was also true of your leaders. But God was fulfilling the prophecies that the Messiah must suffer all of these things. Therefore repent and turn now to God that your sins may be wiped away and that you may know seasons of refreshing (recovery from heat, revival through fresh air) that comes from the presence of the Lord. Then He will send Jesus, your Messiah, back to you again. For He must remain in heaven until the restitution (universal recovery, restoration, reformation, readjustment) of all things which God has spoken by the prophets of old.
>
> Acts 3:17–21 (paraphrased)

Yes, we live in a world which has fallen heir to God's judgment because of man's rebellion, yet there is a future expectation which shall be realized when redeemed man moves into the full power and authority of his Sonship in Christ Jesus. There is a great wonder in these words from the Apostle Paul:

In my opinion whatever we may have to go through now is less than nothing compared with the magnificent future God has planned for us. The whole creation is on tiptoe to see the wonderful sight of the sons of God coming into their own. The world of creation cannot as yet see Reality, not because it chooses to be blind, but because in God's purpose it has been so limited—yet it has been given hope. And the hope is that in the end the whole of created life will be rescued from the tyranny of change and decay, and have its share in that magnificent liberty which can only belong to the children of God! It is plain to anyone with eyes to see that at the present time all created life groans in a sort of universal travail. And it is plain, too, that we who have a foretaste of the Spirit are in a state of painful tension, while we wait for that redemption of our bodies which will mean that at last we have realized our full sonship in Him.

Romans 8:18-23 PHILLIPS

This Is Our Father's World

This is our Father's world, and it is yet to be filled with His glory in Christ Jesus through His family:

And we know that all that happens to us is working for our good if we love God and are fitting into his plans. For from the very beginning God decided that those who came to him —and all along he knew who would—should become like his Son, so that his Son would be the First, with many brothers. And having chosen us, he called us to come to him; and when we came, he declared us "not guilty," filled us with Christ's goodness, gave us right standing with himself, and promised us his glory.

Romans 8:28-30 LB

And we all with unveiled faces—reflecting the glory of the Lord—are being changed into His likeness from one degree of glory to another; for this comes from the Lord who is the Spirit.

2 Corinthians 3:18 (paraphrased)

Arise, my people! Let your light shine for all the nations to see! For the glory of the Lord is streaming from you. Darkness as black as night shall cover all the peoples of the earth, but the glory of the Lord will shine from you. All nations will come to your light; mighty kings will come to see the glory of the Lord upon you.

Isaiah 60:1–3 LB

For the earth shall be filled with the knowledge of the glory of the LORD as the waters cover the sea.

Habakkuk 2:14

It is my opinion that the fulfillment of this glorious hope is not altogether in the far-away future, but is a reality the first fruits of which we can experience now. Martin Luther once said that as Christians we ought to be ready to "risk the glorious."

The Web of Life

Ecology is interested in the balanced relationship that exists between successful species and their living (other species) and nonliving (physical) environments. In other words a given organism must find his place among other living organisms as well as adapt to the physical character of his surroundings.

A given species which exists in a localized area is referred to as a *population*. A town not only has a population of people, but of dogs, cats, rosebushes, elm trees, etc.

All of the populations of different species that live together in a localized area are collectively called a *community*. Usually there is a mutually dependent relationship between the various kinds of organisms which is delicately balanced. This often involves a "food chain."

Green plants (as clover) are designated as *producers* because only they can convert radiant energy into chemical energy by the process of photosynthesis. Animals that subsist on a diet of plants are called *primary consumers* (as rabbits), while animals that prey on other animals (as coyotes) are referred to as *secondary consumers*. The consumer chain could have a long and complicated pattern of connecting links. *Decomposers* (as bacteria and fungi) reduce the dead remains of both plants and animals into chemical components which can again be utilized by the plant producers at the beginning of the food chain.

Living organisms must also be adapted to their physical environment or they will soon perish—like a fish out of water! A living community and its associated physical environment is called an *ecosystem*. This may be a field, park, lake, or tide pool, but the physical features will be fairly consistent in character. Ecosystems can correspondingly change in character with either altitude or latitude. For instance, there is a change in climate from the equator to the poles that corresponds with a similar transition from sea level to the mountaintops. This is reflected in what is described by the biologist as a series of *ecological zones,* which are usually characterized by the kind of vegetation that is dominant. At the bottom of either scale can be found the rain forests. As one proceeds, the transition follows a typical pattern: deciduous forests, coniferous forests, smaller herbs and shrubs, lichens and mosses, and finally the sterile ice caps of the higher polar regions. Each zone, of course, has its own peculiar community of animals that could not readily survive outside its own particular habitat.

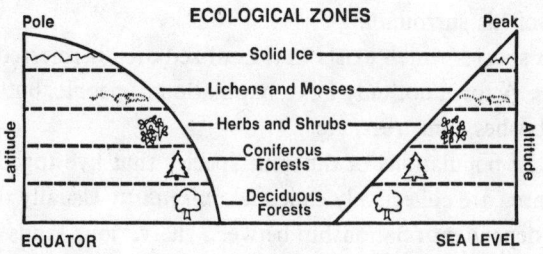

ECOLOGICAL ZONES

Pole — Solid Ice — Peak
Lichens and Mosses
Herbs and Shrubs
Coniferous Forests
Deciduous Forests

Latitude / Altitude
EQUATOR — SEA LEVEL

Each species has a place and a purpose in the web of life. Every organism has a role in, and a position of relationship to, both the living and nonliving environment which is essential to its own well-being and that of the community. This is referred to as its "niche" in the economy of life. To be misplaced or miscast in terms of position or role will only bring limitation to all concerned. There are many tragic examples of man's tinkering with the balance of nature and reaping results far beyond what he could have imagined. The dust bowl in the Midwest during the nineteen thirties is but one example.

There is of course a web of life in the divine economy as well. We all have a role and a place in the Kingdom of God, which corresponds to the truth which we have seen concerning the realm of nature. We each need to find our "niche" and discover how and where we are to relate in a practical, personal way to the balanced order which God has ordained for His people. It is easy to say that for such an hour as this have we come to the Kingdom—but, where are we to be, and what are we to do? There are some spiritual dust bowls to be revived, and some burnt-over fields which desperately need to be cultivated, seeded, weeded, and watered.

Relationship within the life of the Christian community helps provide the direction, protection, and recognition which are necessary for the discovery and development of our personal role and particular responsibility within the Kingdom of God. The fivefold ministries of apostle, prophet, evangelist, pastor, and teacher are listed in the fourth chapter of Ephesians. Other functions are recorded elsewhere: ministry and helps, exhortation, giving, rulership and governments, mercy, miracles and healings (Romans 12:6–8; 1 Corinthians 12:28–29). Many additional ministries are implied throughout Scripture: intercessory prayer, hospitality, visitation, reconciliation, social concern, literature, music, etc. Mission fields include the home, neighborhood, and the worlds of business, academics, science, medicine, athletics, recreation, entertainment, politics, the military, the ghetto, the teenager, the senior citizen, and a host of others. Each of these fields is comprised of individuals united together by common interests, culture, and language, as is true of mission fields, which are usually characterized geographically. (A more detailed discussion is considered in Chapter 9 of the author's book *Set My Spirit Free,* published by Logos International.)

The important principle to follow in discovering our place and function in the royal family of God is to begin where we are, and seek to share the life and love of Jesus with those we find in the mission fields related to our present life situation. Again we are not to despise the day of small things; God works wisely, carefully, patiently, but most persistently in preparing His people for their calling.

There is a danger in trying to assume a place of personal prominence, prestige, and power while concurrently avoiding the character-producing work of the cross, which involves time, testing, and experience within the Christian community. Exposure to the ways and words of God in the living church at large as one matures also brings a balance and a perspective to our ministry within the Kingdom of God. As we have seen in the realm of nature, it is good to recognize the particular role we play as it relates to God's overall plan; otherwise we can become so preoccupied with our place and function in the Kingdom that we lose sight of the larger purpose. If we do, we begin to measure everything and everyone in terms of how it or they will enhance "our" ministry rather than by the contributions they make to the Kingdom as a whole. Ultimately such ministries will become not only self-centered, but also self-limited.

Knowing Our Niche

Another danger in endeavoring to discover and develop our ministries is to assume we have to play every position and cover all of the bases. We need to discover our "niche" and concentrate our time and talent as it relates to God's particular call upon our lives. Otherwise we shall wear ourselves out doing much but accomplishing little in terms of divine priority. Usually this then leads to self-condemnation and frustration.

During a conference overseas, one of the speakers asked if he and his wife might share with me a matter which was of deep concern to him. I was humbled, for he was my senior by many years, and with an overall knowledge of the Word which I knew was superior to mine in many areas. Yet I felt at this particular time, because of some deep inner healings God had brought to my own life, that I might be able to be used of the Lord to reach his point of need.

He readily confessed some areas in his life where he felt his testimony for the Lord was very weak because of deep inferiority feelings. It was very difficult for him to witness directly to strangers. He felt particularly distressed when around evangelists who had developed an aggressive ministry in their outreach endeavors. He even expressed his reluctance to converse with other ministers at get-acquainted gatherings if they too were strangers. His embarrassment was intensified by an uncontrolled stammering which would express itself on such occasions. He was plagued by feelings of guilt and inferiority.

His wife persistently and graciously counterbalanced his depreciating remarks by describing his anointed ministry in teaching and personal counseling. He confessed that in these areas of activity he did have great freedom and was aware of the Lord's blessing upon his own life and those with whom he shared. He obviously was a very wise and loving servant who effectively reached the hearts and lives of God's people in these ways. Yet in spite of all of this he felt he had failed God and was deeply disappointed in his own service for the Lord.

As we continued to share together, he recalled an incident earlier in his ministry which had made an indelible impression upon his heart and mind. A supposedly spiritually minded woman had on one occasion informed him that because he lacked evangelistic zeal in the winning of souls, his ministry was neither complete nor totally acceptable in the eyes of God. She pictured his life as a dam with five sluice gates, of which only one was open. Ever since, that picture had haunted his life and ministry and poisoned his love and faith relationship with the Lord.

It is possible to serve God and see people blessed and still have keen feelings of failure and inferiority. The Enemy effectively directs our attention away from the areas of God's blessing in our ministry and condemns us for not being all things to all men (and women)! I shared with him the many occasions where I had had similar feelings, and without realizing it was totally depreciating God's ministry through my life in spite of encouraging words from others. I remember a friend exhorting me once not to underestimate our ministries in the Lord—because the devil doesn't! We continued to talk about the necessity of knowing our "niche" in God's economy and seriously accepting and appreciating the ministry that God has given us.

Suddenly a light broke across his countenance and he exclaimed, "I think I understand what my problem is. I haven't recognized the boundaries which the Lord has set for my ministry. I have been trying to compete with men whose ministries were quite different from mine in character. As a result, I have actually hindered the development of my own ministry and robbed myself of the joy that is the reward of the worker who faithfully sows and reaps in the field which God has chosen for his labor!"

A great sense of relief and peace filled his life, and we all bore witness to words of wisdom which the Spirit had brought concerning the issue which had been so disturbing. We embraced each other and praised the Lord for the liberty that is the privilege of all who are led of God's Spirit.

As a result of this releasing insight he realized he no longer would need to feel he was competing with anyone, but would recognize and appreciate the ministries of others just as he did his own. Furthermore, should opportunities come to share Jesus with strangers, there would be no feeling of compulsion to follow any particular form or pattern unless he felt at peace to do so. It would be his privilege and joy to warmly and personally relate to them around some area of need or concern, just as God had taught him in his personal counseling with others. Indeed, there was now a new-found boldness to simply be himself in the Lord and restfully follow the promptings of the Holy

Spirit with which he was already familiar. He had discovered his "niche" in the divine web of life!

Succession: The Secret to Success

Occasionally natural disasters can upset the character of a balanced ecosystem or even eliminate it altogether. Community life may be completely destroyed by the devastating forces of floods, wind, and fire. Life is persistent, however, and the barren land will seek in time to recover its original state of existence. This involves a succession of different kinds of communities, as each is dependent upon the preceding for its support and development.

Following a fire which has destroyed a typical deciduous forest, life would begin a process of restoration which would seek to heal the ugly wound that had been inflicted upon mother nature. Scorched soil and barren rocks would support an invasion of lichens, mosses, grasses, and eventually ferns and flowers. Animals and insects suitable for this simple environment would quickly follow. Humble herbs and sturdy shrubs would subsequently appear, as seeds borne by the winds and carried by the birds would find a warm welcome from an earth well on its way to recovery. These pioneer plants would provide the setting in which the larger trees as birches, oaks, and finally maples would grow. The large maple trees would eventually shade over the forest floor and suppress the further growth of other seedling trees as a mature or climax stage ultimately is achieved. Each stage in the process of succession is associated with its own particular community of birds, animals, and insects as ecological maturity is approached.

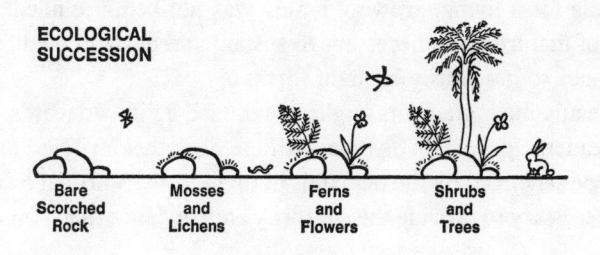

ECOLOGICAL SUCCESSION

Bare Scorched Rock — Mosses and Lichens — Ferns and Flowers — Shrubs and Trees

It is very interesting that the establishment and maturity of Christian communities follow a similar pattern. Perhaps this is most strikingly illustrated by the development of various forms of community life which have grown out of the charismatic renewal movement. Most typical is that associated with the Catholic Pentecostals. It has been my privilege to both observe and participate in this movement for some years.

Whenever lives are truly renewed by the power of the Holy Spirit, there is an associated development and expression of the fruit and gifts of the Spirit. As with the first charismatic community described in the second chapter of Acts, people automatically want to share together with others who are likewise becoming alive to Christ in this new and exciting way. The simplest level of fellowship usually is the informal prayer meeting. Novelty and need are sometimes the main forces of attraction; individuals come together because there is a need and a desire to know and express God's life and love in a real and personal way. Dormant gifts of the Spirit become operational and bring a fresh experience of God's presence. Worship is free and enthusiastic, often associated with new songs sweetly inspired by the Holy Spirit. Prayers are bold and expressed with expectation. There is much joy, praise, and loving concern. The meetings might be characterized as lively but loose.

In time it became apparent that after the novelty wore off or personal needs were met (sometimes miraculously), some would gradually drift back into the indifference which had formerly characterized their lives. Certain members in the groups, to whom the Holy Spirit had given a shepherd's heart, became concerned that God's ongoing purpose for a living, growing family was not being fulfilled. A new level of maturity was necessary to sustain and develop the life which God had so graciously brought forth.

The missing ingredients might be summed up in two words: loyalty and leadership. One involves an attitude, the other an office; and both must be sanctified by the demands of divine love. Spiritual leadership was necessary to provide the authority and guidance that would evoke a sense of loyalty to God and each other that would go beyond the whims of personal needs or desires. Commitment to one another and the Lord, coupled with respect for recognized authority and leadership, would bring a stability to the emerging community that God could bless.

The graces and gifts of the Spirit would take on a higher purpose, for they would be seen as means of preparing personal ministries as different individuals began finding their "niche" within the life of the fellowship. As various ministries developed, the strength, stability, and maturity of the community increased. A corporate voice and working power emerged which had the authority and wisdom that God confers upon a fully functioning expression of the Body of Christ.

The various modes of community life vary as God shapes His people for His purpose in a local situation. The same essential ingredients are always there, however, wherever a healthy, balanced community is developing—loyalty and leadership in love!

Symbiotic Relationships

There are some interesting kinds of "living-together" situations which come under the heading of *symbiosis* (syn-together; bios-life).

PARASITISM refers to a symbiotic relationship in which one member benefits at the expense and even detriment of the other. A parasitic tapeworm, for instance, lives off the nutrients in the intestines of its host. At the same time it realeases toxic by-products which are harmful to its friendly homemaker.

Occasionally a Christian community may harbor individuals with parasitic tendencies. They drain everyone else of his energy, time, and attention and then infect the fellowship with their rebellion, resentment, and self-pity. Such "spiritual leeches" need to be *disciplined* and even removed if there is no response to loving correction. The welfare of the whole body is involved.

COMMENSALISM refers to a symbiotic relationship in which one member benefits, while the other is neither helped nor harmed. There is a little flat worm that attaches itself to the exterior shell of certain crustaceans; here it can feed on food particles which are released as the crab or lobster shreds its meal with its claws. It doesn't really interfere with the life of its host, but it doesn't contribute anything to its welfare either.

Parallels are easy to find within the Christian community. Many turn to the church to be formally christened, baptized, married, and buried, but are otherwise disinterested. Others relate themselves to a Christian fellowship as a source of supply for their emotional and spiritual needs, but never share their blessings with others, either within or without the community. They are what might be called "spiritual sponges," who need to be *directed* into the greater joy of sharing God's grace with others. If not so directed, "commensal" Christians have a tendency to degenerate into "parasitic" Christians.

MUTUALISM is a symbiotic relationship in which each member benefits the other and thereby enhances their common good. The wood-eating termite has no intestinal enzymes with which to digest cellulose, which is the main component in its diet. Fortunately it is the host for an intestinal protozoan (one-celled animal) which does possess such enzymes. The protozoan could not exist outside of the termite's digestive tract, nor could the termite exist without the protozoan's enzyme activity inside its digestive tract. "Togetherness" for them means life; "apartness" means death!

In the economy of spiritual life, of course, commensalism is the ideal relationship between members in the Christian community. There is a *delegation* of responsibilities and privileges which mutually enhances all concerned. We need each other very much, and must be generous enough to give, and humble enough to receive. All of us have probably fallen short on both accounts at one time or another, and need to be balanced in our sharing relationships with each other.

I recall a meeting some years ago which was the last in a series that had been very demanding physically and spiritually for my partner and me. As the final invitation was extended to those who needed prayer and counsel, both of us realized we were exhausted, and in the natural had little left to give. Sometimes God lifts us beyond our limitations in such situations, but this time He had an even better solution in view.

Following a prompting from God's Spirit, we both came around to the front of the communion rail and honestly requested our brothers and sisters in the audience to come forward and pray for us. And come they did—in fact it was one of the better services in the whole series! It was a beautiful and refreshing experience with an obvious lesson which I have never forgotten.

The Sphere of Life

In nature no community exists totally isolated from other communities and the overall economy of life worldwide. The entire film of life which covers the surface of our globe is referred to as the "biosphere." There is a universal relationship in biology that involves the entire order of Creation. Each of the essential cycles for water, carbon, oxygen, and nitrogen passes through phases which involve the atmospheric heavens, the earth, and all living things.

In the process of photosynthesis, for instance, plants link together carbon dioxide from the air, and water from the soil to form large carbon-chain molecules (organic compounds) such as sugar, starch and fat, and protein. One of the by-products of photosynthesis is oxygen, which is immediately released by the plant back into the atmosphere. Plant substance is then converted by "primary consumers" into animal carbohydrates, fats, and protein. Part of these nutrients will be utilized to synthesize animal tissue for growth and repair. The rest, however, is "burned" as fuel to produce the energy necessary to turn the wheels of their metabolic machinery.

The oxygen required for the "burning" process is obtained from the atmosphere by respiration. The by-products of the "burning" process are carbon dioxide and water. The carbon dioxide is released back into the atmosphere, where it is available again to the green plants. After death, animal and plant organic remains are almost completely converted back into carbon dioxide and water by "decomposers" (bacteria, fungi) and the cycle is complete. Should plants stop photosynthesizing and decomposers stop decomposing, the cycles would essentially be broken; carbon and oxygen would become "fixed" in the remains of dying creatures, and eventually the whole earth would become a graveyard cluttered with undecomposed bodies!

INTERRELATED CHEMICAL CYCLES ESSENTIAL FOR LIFE —

Photosynthesis / Respiration

CO_2 O_2 → O_2 CO_2 → → O_2 CO_2

H_2O / H_2O / Death / H_2O

Plant: Organic Nutrients | Rabbit: Primary Consumer | Bacteria and Fungi: Decomposers

One obviously senses the significance of mutual dependence in the overall scheme of life. No organism or community of organisms can live a totally isolated or independent existence for very long. The same is true in regard to our individual and community life in the Spirit. A balanced, healthy existence spiritually involves relationship. This is one reason that Jesus prayed that we would become one. The Holy Spirit is moving to bring healing to the Body of Christ in our day in a way that has never before been witnessed in all of history. There is a "biosphere" in the spiritual realm as in the natural. It comprises all of God's people over the face of the earth who have entered into life relationship with the Lord Jesus Christ as their Brother-Redeemer. It is a relationship which includes all of our brothers and sisters in the family of God. Gradually wounds and scars are being healed and covered over, that together we may present a convincing witness of God's life and love to the whole wide world.

Pollution and Poverty

The interrelated problems of pollution and conservation of our natural resources have captured the attention of an ecology-minded world. Both issues have been aggravated by the population and knowledge explosions which are related to our generation. Advances in technology, designed to meet the wants and needs of an increasing population, have produced by-products of pollution sufficient to suffocate man in his own smoke, or bury him in his own waste.

The problem of pollution and poverty in the realm of nature is but a reflection of a greater pollution and poverty within the soul of man. Attempts to solve the external problems are ultimately doomed to failure if the inner problem is left untouched. Our Heavenly Father knows that we have been fashioned from the dust of this earth, and apart from His Holy Spirit we are doomed to death and decay—both within and without. We have been soiled by the sin of our own self-willed ways, and the corruption of our souls has finally infected the world in which we live. The problems of pollution and poverty (resource exhaustion) are directly the result of shortsighted, self-centered men, who have sought their own pleasure and profit regardless of the price that ultimately must be paid by both creature and creation. It is a policy which works for a while but eventually produces diminishing returns, and ultimately makes a demand of its own —with interest!

The only answer to moral pollution is inner purification! It is not without particular significance that the redeeming Spirit of God is referred to as "Holy" Ghost. He not only convicts men of their sin but desires to cleanse them from its contaminating influence as well. This is accomplished as God's Holy Spirit continually washes us with God's Holy Word—Jesus is that Living Word!

> Christ loved the Church and gave Himself for her that He might sanctify her with the washing of water with the Word, that He might present the Church to Himself in glorious

splendor without stain, wrinkle, or any such things—that she might be holy and faultless before Him.

Ephesians 5:25-27 (paraphrased)

And now, Father . . . sanctify them (make them holy) through Your Word; Your Word is truth.

John 17:5, 17 (paraphrased)

Now ye are clean through the word which I [Jesus] have spoken unto you.

John 15:3

You have purified your souls in obeying the truth through the Holy Spirit.

1 Peter 1:22 (paraphrased)

Do not be deceived; neither the impure and immoral, nor idolators, nor adulterers, nor homosexuals, nor thieves, nor the greedy, nor drunkards, nor the foul-mouthed, nor the swindler will inherit the Kingdom of God. And such were some of you: but you were washed, you were sanctified, you were justified in the name of the Lord Jesus Christ and in the Spirit of our God.

1 Corinthians 6:9-11 (paraphrased)

In the Sermon on the Mount, Jesus was describing the responsibility and mission which subjects in the Kingdom of God were to have in a world polluted by sin: "You are the salt of the earth!" In other words, Christians—individually and collectively—are to exert a cleansing, purifying, and preserving influence in their social environment. Salt without its strength, Jesus declares, is worthless, as far as concerns the arresting and reversing of the processes of decay and corruption (Matthew 5:13). The same is true of a Christian without the cleansing work of the cross or the purifying power of the Holy Spirit in his life. Our own hearts must be clean before God's holy purpose can be accomplished through our lives.

The Psalmist through inspired poetry speaks to our soul from his as he shares his deepest thoughts and feelings concerning inner holiness of heart:

> O loving and kind God, have mercy. Have pity upon me and take away the awful stain of my transgressions. Oh, wash me, cleanse me from this guilt. Let me be pure again. . . . Sprinkle me with the cleansing blood and I shall be clean again. Wash me and I shall be whiter than snow. . . . Create in me a new, clean heart, O God, filled with clean thoughts and right desires. Don't toss me aside, banished forever from your presence. Don't take your Holy Spirit from me. Restore to me again the joy of your salvation, and make me willing to obey you. Then I will teach your ways to other sinners, and they—guilty like me—will repent and return to you.
>
> Psalms 51:1–2, 7, 10–13 LB

Our life for the Lord will be greatly limited in reaching others with the cleansing power of His love if we ourselves are under a heavy burden of guilt or condemnation. Many Christians are still haunted by the past and cannot really accept God's forgiveness—let alone forgive themselves.

Created: One Clean Heart

While writing this very chapter, I received a long-distance phone call from a minister of the Gospel who through a moral lapse in his life was suffering the torments of continual condemnation by the Accuser. He had repeatedly repented for his transgression, and had earnestly sought God for forgiveness. His great heart's desire was to serve the Lord again in the ministry of His Word, but he was haunted by the fear that he might have committed the unpardonable sin. His faithful wife repeatedly assured him of her love, and with him had prayed that he might be restored to the joy of his salvation. His only relief came when he would stand behind the pulpit and proclaim the Holy Word of God. Immediately thereafter he would again come under condemnation, and feel that he had gone beyond God's grace.

I have discovered from the response to many inquiries that some sixty to seventy percent of the people in my audiences feel that at one time or another in their Christian experience they may have crossed God's line of grace, and that He finally had given up on them! I usually have the people raise their hands as an indication and then encourage them all to look around and see the host of hands that has joined theirs. For some, I am sure, this was the first time they had ever shared their particular concern with anyone. Condemnation seems to be one of Satan's favorite weapons. Should a reader find himself suffering from a similar shadow in his past, there is good news to follow!

I assured the minister who had called that I knew how he felt, for I and many others had known what it was to have the Accuser point his sinister finger of condemnation in our direction. It took some time to assure him from God's Word, and by the convincing witness of the Holy Spirit in his own heart, that he could never turn off God's love, regardless of what he had been or done. Those who have committed the unpardonable sin have such hardened hearts and seared consciences that they no longer are interested in the love of God—but even then it is still there, for it is everlasting in character. We may reject His love, but we cannot turn it off!

We spent some time talking about the forgiving, healing, and redeeming power in the blood of Jesus, which was shed for our sins. There is no stain of sin or pollution of soul which cannot be cleansed by the cross of Jesus Christ. He kept pleading for the hope of forgiveness, yet felt the persistent pull of the Adversary to doubt the goodness and greatness of God's grace. We finally rebuked the spirit of condemnation, confessed the Lordship of Jesus, and pronounced on the authority of God's Word that, in the name of our Saviour and through the cleansing power of His blood, God had put away his sin;

and he was forgiven—now and forever!

I heard a cry of joy on the other end of the phone, followed by profuse praise and thanksgiving in a beautiful language of the Spirit, and there was no doubt about it—Jesus had done it again!

"He whom the Son sets free is free indeed!"

I could sense he felt as if he had just taken a bath—inside and out. There is no "cleaner" feeling in all the world than to know that our sins have been put away, and that the pure, clear streams of God's Holy Spirit have scrubbed our souls to a whiteness as bright as the snow.

> Come now, and let us reason together, saith the LORD: though your sins be as scarlet, they shall be as white as snow; though they be red like crimson, they shall be as wool.
>
> Isaiah 1:18

Ecology of the Eternal

Yes, a holy life on earth in time is our preparation for the purity of heaven in eternity. The ecology of the eternal state exhibits a beautiful balance where all of life will be in harmony with God's holy and glorious plan for His beloved family:

> For see, I am creating new heavens and a new earth—so wonderful that no one will even think about the old ones anymore. Be glad; rejoice forever in my creation. Look! I will recreate Jerusalem as a place of happiness, and her people shall be a joy! . . . The wolf and lamb shall feed together, the lion shall eat straw as the ox does, and poisonous snakes shall strike no more! . . . Nothing will hurt or destroy in all my holy mountain, for as the waters fill the sea, so shall the earth be full of the knowledge of the Lord.
>
> Isaiah 65:17–18, 25; 11:9 LB

And He showed me a pure river whose waters give life, sparkling like crystal, flowing out from the throne of God and of the Lamb, and down the middle of the main street of the city (the New Jerusalem). On either side of the river stood the Tree of Life, bearing twelve fruits, a different kind for each month. The leaves of the tree were for the healing of the nations. There shall no longer exist anything that is accursed—detestable, foul, offensive, impure, hateful, or horrible; for the throne of God and of the Lamb shall be there, and His servants shall worship Him—forever and ever!

Revelation 22:1–3 (paraphrased)

6
The What of Life

How do we determine whether something is alive or dead, living or nonliving? There are many common "signs" of life which we take for granted. The lusty cry of a ruddy-faced newborn baby is a welcome sight and sound that brings joy and delight to those who have patiently waited for the lively arrival. A box of growing puppies is filled with warm wiggles and soft whimpering sounds, as little balls of fur with empty stomachs crawl all over each other in search of their supper. The sweet fresh fragrance of orange blossoms fills the air with a perfumed promise of a fruitful year. The physician's trained eye, ear, and hand seek out the "vital signs" of cardiac, respiratory, and reflex activity that indicate these essential functions of life are still present in a patient who is critically ill. The indications of death are equally obvious. Usually the evidence is offensive to all of our senses. Rotten eggs and apples are quick to let us know that life has long since made its departure. The cold, still carcass of a little rabbit upon the mountain trail, or even the faded colors, fallen petals, and wilted leaves of a once lovely bouquet all leave us with a certain sense of sadness, for we are aware that these are the familiar signs of death.

The Mysterious Boundary Between Life and Death

The boundary between the living and the nonliving is not always so obvious, however. The crusty little gray lichen mentioned in the previous chapter doesn't look very lively at all unless examined microscopically. Seeds recovered from one of the ancient tombs in the

Middle East were thought to be lifeless until it was discovered that they would germinate when planted!

In higher organisms, life and death are expressed at various levels. Our bodies are composed of cells and their products which in turn form the four basic tissues of life: epithelia (covering-lining), connective tissue (fibrous-cartilage-bone), muscular, and nervous. The organs are constructed from the primary tissues, and themselves contribute to the formation of the organ systems (circulatory, respiratory, digestive, etc.).

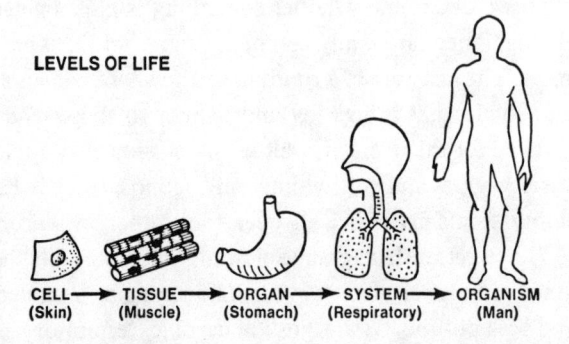

LEVELS OF LIFE

CELL ➔ TISSUE ➔ ORGAN ➔ SYSTEM ➔ ORGANISM
(Skin)   (Muscle)   (Stomach)   (Respiratory)   (Man)

Experimental studies have been performed in physiology utilizing heart-lung preparations which have been removed from the body of an anesthetized animal. The animal's carcass is incinerated, and life at the level of the organism has been destroyed; yet at the heart-lung organ level, function can be independently maintained for some time.

A more striking example involves the Hela strain of cells, which has been utilized in tissue-culture studies for over two decades in laboratories throughout the world. The strain was named after Henrietta Lake, who in the late forties had a biopsy performed because of suspected cancer. The results were positive and she died shortly thereafter. Some of the biopsy cells, however, were tissue cultured and grew profusely. Since then they have been subcultured countless times and the strain is still alive today. Life has been maintained at the cellular level—although as an individual

Henrietta Lake has been gone for over twenty years!

What are the basic characteristics of life that all living things have in common? What qualities of existence disappear when the last flicker from the flame of life is extinguished and dynamic creaturehood is reduced to the dust whence it came? What combination of vital functions is always found wherever and however life may be expressed? There is a diversity in the display of living things which ranges from the minute microorganisms observed in a tiny drop of pond water to the mighty mammoths discovered only in the oceanic depths; yet, each shares the same basic combination of functions which characterize life as we know it. What are they?

The Functional Characteristics of Life

Biologists have discovered that all living things *metabolize* and *perpetuate* themselves. These two essential features each involve several interesting functions, which are outlined below:

I. METABOLISM
Includes all of the internal physical and chemical processes which sustain life.
   A. *Nutrition:* Ingestion, digestion, and transfer of cellular nutrients.
   B. *Respiration:* Chemical process by which energy is released from those nutrients which are "burned" as fuel. This is the internal power source for all the functions of life.
   C. *Synthesis:* Chemical process by which the remaining nutrients are "built" into the structure of cells and their products. Note: Energy for synthesis also comes from the above process of respiration.

II. SELF-PRESERVATION
Includes the various means by which life is extended for the individual and the species.

A. *Steady-state controls:* Compensating functions and disease-defense mechanisms by which the internal environment is maintained in a state which is compatible with life. (Examples: regulation of temperature, acid-base balance, salt concentration, hormone, antibody, and nutrient levels, etc.).
B. *Reproduction:* Nature's way of outwitting death at the level of the individual organism. It involves either simple cell division or the production of reproductive units such as sex cells or spores. The parent organisms may die, but life is continued through their offspring.
C. *Adaptation:* Nature's way of outwitting death at the level of the species. This involves the ability of the species to favorably change with its environment through successive generations rather than becoming extinct. The extent to which adaptation is possible is determined in part upon the genetic (heredity) potential of the species in question.

In summary then: Nutrition, respiration, synthesis, steady-state controls, reproduction, and adaptation are functional characteristics which all living things share in common.

We Are What We Eat!

What rich, penetrating insight such understanding concerning the characteristics of natural life brings to our life in the Spirit. Nutritionalists have repeatedly informed us that "we are what we eat." Bodily form and function are determined by the quantity and quality of our daily food. Without the proper amount, our bodies become weak and literally waste away; without the proper quality, we soon succumb to the divers diseases of malnutrition. Improper diet in the natural stunts our growth, softens our bones, weakens our muscles, depletes our energy reserves, destroys our defense mechanisms, and reduces our reproductive potential!

Several years ago someone shared with me a personal story of inner healing which beautifully illustrates how the natural principles of nutrition, as they relate to full form and function, also apply to our life in the Spirit. A lady had come to a prayer-and-share group seeking deliverance from fear and depression which had paralyzed her personality and crippled her mental and emotional faculties. Contrary to her expectations, no specific prayers of deliverance were offered. Perhaps her plea had been recognized in part as a patterned response which avoided the responsibility that God desired she personally assume in achieving a thorough and lasting release.

She was assured, however, that her brothers and sisters in Christ would stand with her in prayer and loving concern. She also was encouraged to participate in her own deliverance by faithfully and obediently following a prescription which had been wisely prompted by the Holy Spirit. She was instructed to read the Scriptures and to pray and praise God whether she felt like it or not. She was encouraged to daily share the love of Jesus with someone, even if it was just a smile or a cup of cold water in His name. Communion and fellowship with her brothers and sisters in Christ were also recognized as absolutely essential for her recovery and continued well-being.

She carefully and faithfully followed the counsel which had been offered to her, and a miracle of deliverance was set in motion. She had a lovely voice but was always reluctant and fearful about ministering anywhere in song. With encouragement, she began to worship more freely with the family of God and, on occasion, even to sing songs of praise as a blessing for the fellowship. Over the succeeding weeks the cold gray clouds of fear and depression gave way to the rosy mists of the morning as "the Sun of Righteousness arose with healing in His wings." The dark night of her soul finally surrendered to the inevitable and glorious dawning of a new day—filled with the promise of His abiding peace and joy. The Christ of her life had set her free!

Starve Your Gorilla to Death

A short time after her new-found release, the Lord gave her an unusual dream. It seemed she was in the kitchen of her home, and chancing to glance through the curtained window, she saw the remains of a huge gorilla which had been chained in her back yard. Little now was left but a shriveled form of hide, hair, and bones; she realized the ugly creature had *starved* to death!

By confessing the Lordship of our Christ in the power of the Holy Spirit, the Adversary of our souls can be bound and his access to our lives restrained. Jesus promised us power over all the power of our enemies; we are not helpless, hopeless victims of Satan (and his demonic forces), of self (our old sin nature/flesh), or even of people with overpowering personalities. We need not be controlled by our negative attitudes, unwholesome appetites, unpredictable moods, destructive habits, enervating compulsions, and paralyzing fears. Whatever the nature of our "gorilla," it can be bound on the authority of God's Word and in the name of Jesus Christ our Lord!

> If therefore the Son shall make you free, you shall be free indeed.
>
> John 8:36 NAS

> Behold, I have given you authority to tread upon serpents and scorpions, and over all the power of the enemy, and nothing shall injure you.
>
> Luke 10:19 NAS

> So, dear brothers, you have no obligations whatever to your old sinful nature to do what it begs you to do. For if you keep on following it you are lost and will perish, but if through the power of the Holy Spirit you crush it and its evil deeds, you shall live. For all who are led by the Spirit of God are sons of God.
>
> Romans 8:12–14 LB

For God has said, "I will never, *never* fail you nor forsake you." That is why we can say without any doubt or fear, "The Lord is my Helper and I am not afraid of anything that mere man can do to me."

Hebrews 13:5, 6 LB

The Enemy, however, is a poor loser, and while he no longer can overpower us, he will endeavor to deceive us into coming within the length of his chain. We should not be surprised as we go about our daily affairs in the kitchen to hear the sound of gravel thrown at our backyard window. This is an attention-getting device which hopefully will once again fix our gaze upon the gorilla. The sight we see is designed to draw us out of the kitchen and into the backyard, where we will come within the range of his grasp. He may present himself as a harmless, lovable creature—like a cuddly teddy bear in the zoo—hoping we will be enticed to come out and play, thereby feeding him with our time and attention. On the other hand, he may behave in just the opposite way by roaring, snarling, and pounding his chest, thinking he can intimidate us by a fearful display of power and force. If we yield to such threatening thoughts and feelings, we will soon be drawn back again into the circle of his control.

In a sense, the thoughts and feelings which surround such backyard antics become our daily bread as we give them our time and attention. Such contaminated fare produces an inner sickness of soul which leaves one spiritually weak and exhausted. Our own life is drained and actually becomes the sustenance and strength of the very creature we wish to starve.

We all have gorillas of various sizes, shapes, and colors in the backyard of our lives. God has given the Body of Christ the power and authority to bind the "strong man" that we might be free from his control and influence! It then becomes our obligation to immediately pull down the window blind whenever we hear the familiar sound of gravel on the window. Jesus said if our foot offends us, to cut it off (Mark 9:45-47). He was referring to our responsibility in quickly and decisively dealing with poisonous thoughts and feelings which arise from indulging our backyard captives. Some of us are tempted to give our gorilla one more look, or one last little pat on the head, only to find that one such permissive act leads to a succession of similar decisions, and before we know it we have again left the kitchen for the backyard.

There is a positive side to the picture as well. Jesus said that He stands at the door and knocks; if we would hear and heed His voice He would come in to us and eat with us, and we with Him (Revelation 3:20). There is a sense in which, as we minister to Him, He becomes strong in us; and as He ministers to us, we become strong in Him. In the meantime our gorilla is slowly starving to death! No wonder he is upset by the love and attention we give to our Heavenly Guest, for he can no longer feed upon our lives as was once his privilege and pleasure.

Give Us This Day Our Daily Bread

Jesus said that He was the Bread of Life. This Living Bread is of unusual quality, for it produces the very nature of God within the lives of those who partake of it. This wonderful Bread from heaven brings forgiveness, for it is God's nature to forgive; with it comes healing, for it is God's nature to heal; deliverance from depression will follow, for it is God's nature to deliver; broken hearts and shattered hopes can be mended, for it is God's nature to restore; wasted lives can be reclaimed, for it is God's nature to redeem. What a glorious and gracious provision of divine life and love has been offered to us in Christ Jesus—the Living Bread from heaven!

How do we receive and partake of this Living Bread? The inspired instructions prescribed for the lady mentioned above provide a practical outline concerning the appropriation of Christ's life for our needs and problems:

Prayer

To converse with God activates a line of communication by which our lives are presented and exposed to the vitality of His divine love, wisdom, and power. One definition of "communication" includes the idea of sharing together in a sympathetic and meaningful relationship with someone we love and trust. God knows and understands us better than we know and understand ourselves—and He loves us anyway. We can never shock the Lord by anything we have ever said, done, or been. He truly has been tempted as have we and is therefore touched by the feeling of our infirmities (Hebrews 4:15).

I once questioned the Lord about the extent of His identification with us in our weakness and failures. I wondered if, as the sinless Son of God, He really knew what it was like to fail repeatedly and feel the guilt, rejection, and hopelessness of a life crippled by sin and self-centeredness. He responded lovingly, but very firmly, by informing me that what He had not experienced in His life, He did in His death. When the pure, holy, sinless Son of God took upon Himself our sin and its full consequences, He drank the bitter cup to its very last drop. There was nothing more that could be laid upon His life—He had finished it all—the penalty had been paid in full! (2 Corinthians 5:21).

Yes, He knows and cares about you. The cross was a very personal and desperate expression of His love and willingness to fully identify with us all. For that reason there is no way you can ever shock the Lord Jesus; He has already been there—and much more!

Not only does Jesus know our every need, but His love and compassion is an extension of the Father's care and concern. The Father is not some stern, distant figure whose wrath towards mankind can be averted only by the pleas of Jesus on our behalf. The Father is not the accuser of God's people, Satan is (Revelation 12:10). It was the love of the Father that sent Jesus to a sick and dying world, because of its waywardness and sin. Jesus absorbed that sin and its consquences that we might have free access to the life and love of the Father. In fact, His *is* the life and love of the Father. Our Father God loves us—and

Jesus is the living, loving proof of that truth!

A student of mine who had never known a father's love in an earthly way had difficulty in coming to her Heavenly Father in prayer —Jesus was much easier for her to approach! Patiently, tenderly, and wisely, the Father through the Holy Spirit began to reveal His love to her through Christ Jesus. She came to see that as Jesus drew the little children close to His bosom and lovingly carressed and blessed them, this was a portrait of her Heavenly Father. As she expressed it, it was like the dawning of a new day when she realized that her Father-God really wanted to set her on His lap and put His arms around her and hug her close to His loving heart. As you might imagine, a rather dramatic change occurred in her prayer life. No wonder Jesus said that as earthly children come to their fathers when hungry for bread, we too can confidently come to our Heavenly Father for our daily bread, which He graciously provides through the ministries of His Holy Spirit (Luke 11:1-13).

We continually need to be reminded of our Father's love. Just a few days ago I faced a series of decisions which were interdependent upon one another. I was frustrated and distressed, since many involved letters which were waiting to be answered; yet God's will was not clear concerning some of the initial steps. I carefully explained to the Lord I was willing to take any direction He would indicate, but I couldn't make a move until He revealed His will. Now all of this was true, of course, and really nothing my Heavenly Father didn't already know. In a way my prayer was a proper prayer, but the attitude behind it was not. I had what you might call an "I can't—You won't—therefore You are to blame" complex which was disconnecting me from God's gracious response. I finally picked up the correcting signals from the Holy Spirit, and recognized my faithless lament for what it was. I confessed to the Lord my honest regret for doubting His willingness to lead me into His will if I would restfully trust Him. As He restored His peace within, I happened to glance at an invitation on my desk to visit a regional booksellers' convention which was beginning that very day. I sensed when it had arrived earlier that I was to go, but had forgotten about it. Prompted by this gracious reminder from the Lord, I got dressed and proceeded to the convention center. From the moment I arrived, I watched God—through people whom I never expected to meet—bring to my many needs one divine answer after another. He even answered some questions I hadn't asked! Once again I was reminded that inspired prayers and their answers are very real ways in which we can receive of His life just when we need to live it the most.

> Let us therefore come boldly and confidently to the throne of His grace that we might find mercy for our failures, and grace to help in the hour of our need.
>
> Hebrews 4:16 (paraphrased)

Praise

We are informed by Scripture that God inhabits (lives, dwells in) the praises of His people (Psalms 22:3). In this beautiful Messianic psalm the writer, anticipating the Passion of our Lord, speaks of the confidence we can place in God during dark times of travail and anguish. Though we may feel forsaken, yet He is faithful and worthy of our praise. On the far side of our "shadowed valley" is the bright glory of God's resurrection power. We can draw upon the strength of that power while we are still within the valley.

There is a life in praise which can "restore our souls" during times of stress and strain that would otherwise tempt us to feed our gorillas of pessimism, despair, and self-pity. Often I will awaken at night and spend time in prayer regarding our family, ministry for the Lord, our nation, etc. Sometimes, however, I have noticed that I will become preoccupied with the problem or need around which I am praying until it assumes more importance than the One to whom I am addressing my prayer! This is the time for "problem-prayer" to shift to "praise-prayer." In praising God our perspective shifts heavenward again; our attitude becomes positive, and the Lord can anoint our "heads" (thought life) with the soothing oil of the Holy Spirit, and strengthen our inner man from the banquet table which He bountifully spreads before us—even in the presence of our enemies.

As we praise God for who He is, and what He has done, the Holy Spirit has a basis for His blessing. He cannot bless a confession that does not honor the worthiness of God. Furthermore, one doesn't have to feel like praising God to engage in praise, for He is worthy and faithful regardless of how we feel. In one sense it is not a matter of whether we are going to express praise, but to whom it is going to be directed. Either we will be praising our Heavenly Guest within, or we will be praising the gorilla without!

I had a student some years ago who faithfully cataloged and rehearsed all of his many complaints and problems whenever we met. At first I would fervently pray and try to encourage him in the Lord. After a time I realized there was something sinister about his conduct and conversation which was fruitlessly taking my time and energy. The next time he dropped by my office with another chapter from his book of lamentations, I heard myself spontaneously suggest that since he had spent considerable time praising the devil, we might turn the record over and try praising the Lord. He reacted rather violently by slamming the door and walking out. He came back later, somewhat subdued, and with a willingness to hear what God was trying to teach him about the soul-destroying power of pessimism. It is a deadly poison to our spiritual system! Ultimately the faithful Holy Spirit of love and joy washed away his melancholy moods, and he has become a stable leader among the young people converted from the drug culture.

I have had my wife occasionally run the same routine through with me when I have started a downward spiral of negative thinking. "Why don't we try praising the Lord?" does trigger off a "door-slamming" impulse—never carried through, of course, but detectable nevertheless. The desire to praise God is one of the most sensitive barometers of our spiritual condition. It also is a powerful remedy for the misery of the "poor me" syndrome. Real praise, it must be said, is never a "method" or a "gimmick" that magically converts a rocky road into a path of roses. Praise *does* put us in a position of faith, whereby we are ready to receive more of the Lord's life. Praise also makes us more sensitive to the promptings of His Spirit. His ministry of inner healing may begin with a sense of quietness or rest. The next fruit of the Spirit may be patience, with peace and hope, which enables us to align our steps with His. In this way we can wait without frustration if God slows His pace or even pauses for a time, for we are assured He does all things well. In a way, praise acts as a very effective tranquilizer, yet without depressing the vital flow of His life to ours.

Always be full of joy in the Lord; I say it again, rejoice! ... Don't worry about anything; instead, pray about everything; tell God your needs and don't forget to thank him for his answers. If you do this you will experience God's peace, which is far more wonderful than the human mind can understand. His peace will keep your thoughts and your hearts quiet and at rest as you trust in Christ Jesus.

Philippians 4:4–7 LB

The Word of God

Another way we can receive the life of Jesus is through the inspired reading of Holy Scriptures. Jesus once said that His words were *Spirit* and they were *life* (John 6:63). The Word of God is also declared to be quick (alive) and powerful—energizing in its effect (Hebrews 4:12 AMPLIFIED). The Prophet Jeremiah poetically puts it in this way:

Thy words were found and I ate them, and Thy words became for me a joy and the delight of my heart.

Jeremiah 15:16 NAS

I have always been fascinated by the account of the two grief-stricken disciples on the road to Emmaus following the Resurrection of Jesus. The Lord Himself appeared and engaged them in conversation as they walked along. They did not recognize Him, but listened intently to His exposition of the Scriptures concerning the Christ. Later as He prayed and broke bread with them, their eyes were opened, and they recognized their unusual companion as the Lord. After His miraculous departure, they began to share with one another their feelings about the words He spoke:

> Were not our hearts burning within us while He was speaking to us on the road, while He was explaining the Scriptures to us?
>
> Luke 24:32 NAS

One of the striking features of this story is related to the change of heart which occurred as the inspiring words which Jesus spoke were received by their inner spirit and subconscious soul. At the outset the record describes the disciples as being sad and downcast—in other words, heavyhearted. Jesus dispelled their sadness by ministering words to them concerning Himself. With His words went His life, and they felt the healing fire of His Holy Spirit deep within. Both their heads and their hearts were reached, for their understanding was enlightened and their affections were stirred. The bread that He broke while together with them at the table was symbolic of the Heavenly Bread upon which they had been feasting while walking on the road. They had indeed been strengthened in their inner selves, for following their earthly meal, they immediately returned to Jerusalem (the city of sorrow which they had been fleeing) and enthusiastically shared their experience with the other apostles.

The same holy excitement and healing fire of God's Word can be experienced wherever and whenever it is presented and received in the power of the Holy Spirit. Earlier today I was video-taping a teaching series at a local Christian television station. At the end of the first half-hour session, one of the staff informed me that a gentleman had arrived and desperately wanted prayer. He was ill physically, depressed mentally, and needed the overflowing power of the Holy Spirit. My first reaction was one of concern timewise, for I had four half-hour sessions yet to tape. I have learned, however, that what may seem to be an interruption in my schedule in the natural can often be a divine appointment.

As the staff and I gathered around him for prayer, it was obvious he first needed to be reached with the faith-producing power of God's living Word. Paraphrasing Scripture, we confessed the presence of Jesus in our midst, and the authority He had given us in releasing the power of God's promises concerning our needs. Together we all prayed that God that very moment would perform His Word, and flood his life with the healing, releasing power of the Holy Spirit. With the word of our confession went the inner fire of God's Spirit, and praise and joy began to rise to the lips of one of God's dearest children. A moment later he was lost in the wonder of worship as the Holy Spirit lifted him beyond the limitations of an earthly language and gave him a glorious song in a heavenly tongue (Acts 2:4; Ephesians 5:18–19). Needless to say, the next taping session possessed a freshness of God's Spirit that made the written Word become alive in a very personal way.

As God performs His Word in our lives through the power of the Holy Spirit, the miracle-mystery of the Incarnation is repeated—the Word once more becomes flesh. Heavenly Bread is freshly broken and again brings life to those of God's children who are hungry-hearted.

> And the Word became flesh, and dwelt among us, and we beheld His glory. . . .
> John 1:14 NAS

> I am the living bread that came down out of heaven; if any one eats of this bread, he shall live forever; and the bread also which I shall give for the life of the world is My flesh.
> John 6:51 NAS

> As the Father has sent Me, so send I you . . . receive the Holy Spirit.
>
> John 20:21-22 (paraphrased)
>
> Everyone can see that you are an open letter (epistle) from Christ, written by us; not with pen and ink, but by the Spirit of the living God—not carved on stone, but in human hearts —the Word made flesh.
>
> 2 Corinthians 3:3 (paraphrased)

Fellowship

The Spirit of Christ is ever with *each* believer, for we have the promise that He will never leave us nor forsake us (Matthew 28:20). There is a special purpose to His presence, however, when Christians come *together* in His name; there is a personal impartation of His life that can be received in no other way. There are times, as mentioned in the previous section, when the Word must be personified before it can readily be received into our lives. On such occasions we need to come within reach of our brothers and sisters in Christ before His life in them can touch us with its releasing power.

In our technologically oriented society, which is steadily moving towards reducing individuals to nameless numbers, the wholesome and healing power of neighborly love and concern has almost reached the point of extinction for some who live lonely, even desperate, lives. The population explosion and urban concentration have crowded people together physically, but often isolated them personally, as busy schedules place a premium on privacy. The deterioration of divine purpose in the home and for the family has left many with crippled lives and scarred memories. Faulty or deficient relationships with parents or other family members can carry over into our relationships with our Heavenly Father and with our brothers and sisters in Christ.

Several years ago my wife and I were invited to share in a home prayer meeting in the Los Angeles area. Everyone arrived with a sense of expectation and the room was soon filled with spontaneous songs and prayers of praise and worship. As various needs were expressed, prayers of petition and thanksgiving were offered in a gracious personal way. Suddenly three men left the room. A moment later I was asked to come quickly and join with them in prayer, for one of the men was on the verge of an epileptic seizure. He had felt uneasy during the earlier part of the meeting and recognized the familiar signs which always preceded an attack. He sat tensely huddled over the edge of the bed as if steeling himself against some unseen power. Together we confessed the releasing, healing power of Christ on behalf of our afflicted brother. As we prayed, he began to relax, straighten up, and finally he joined with us in joyful praise to God for his healing.

He then related to us his reluctance to receive prayer for his physical need prior to that time. He had been taught by his father—a rugged man with an iron will—to be totally self-sufficient, and never to look to anyone for help. "Don't be a weak crybaby, but always stand on your own two feet, and take it like a man!" Consequently, it had been hard for him to ever receive anything from anybody. Even after entering into a new life-and-power relationship with Christ in the Holy Spirit, it had still been difficult to submit to others in the family of God for spiritual help of any kind. It took a forced situation related to his physical need to release him from an artificial attitude of self-sufficiency, which had long kept him from receiving the Bread of Life that is graciously offered in the Body of Christ through prayer.

There is an almost mystical element which pervades the oriental customs of hospitality in the Middle East. To lie at table and break bread together involves a communion and commitment of life which goes far beyond our Western concept of entertainment. When within the confines of the host's home or the borders of his tent, a guest is graciously given every provision he may need for his physical welfare and personal protection. The host personally will back this pledge even at the cost of his own life.

There is a special provision and protection which can only be found within the household of God. To exclude ourselves from fellowship in the Body of Christ is to expose ourselves to serious danger and spiritual deprivation. The pathway of life leads us through "shadowed valleys" of various descriptions, but for every valley there is an appropriate banquet table, and a special personal anointing (Psalm 23). Surely this is a reference to our *"abiding* in Christ" and the provisions of His grace. I wonder, however, if there might not be an added meaning that relates to the security and satisfaction that can only be experienced as we find our place within the fellowship of the Father's family. There are many mansions (dwelling places) in our Father's house, and occupancy need not wait for some future time. As we function in fellowship with brothers and sisters in Christ, we in effect are taking up our abode in the house of the Lord. There is a generous anointing and the command of God's blessing when we submit to one another in faith and love and dwell together in unity (Psalm 133). As our cups overflow with His life-giving goodness and mercy we will be able to refresh one another in the Lord, regardless of the darkness and danger which future valleys may hold. We all need each other very much, for only together can we truly face the future with faith and confidence. The good bread of fellowship in Christ is a gracious provision of the Lord's mercy and love for our lives—now and forever!

> Surely goodness, mercy and unfailing love shall follow me all the days of my life; and I shall dwell in the house of the Lord forever.
>
> Psalms 23:6 (paraphrased)

Service to Others

At first glance it would not seem that one of the ways to receive more of Christ's life is by giving away what little we may now think we have of Him. But, Jesus Himself was the one who said:

> Give, and it will be given to you; good measure, pressed down, shaken together, running over, they will pour into

your lap. For whatever measure you deal out *to others,* it will be dealt to you in return.

Luke 6:38 NAS

Paul illustrates the principle by comparing it with the law of increase that motivates the sower:

> He which soweth sparingly shall reap also sparingly; and he which soweth bountifully shall reap also bountifully.
>
> 2 Corinthians 9:6

We are also assured by the natural laws of heredity that life begets life after its own kind. If we plant a field with wheat seed, we don't expect to harvest a crop of elephants! We know from practical experience that such a suggestion is utterly absurd. Somehow, however, it is difficult to carry the same principles over into our life in the Spirit. Some of us on occasion have expected a happy harvest from a field that was never sown with good grain.

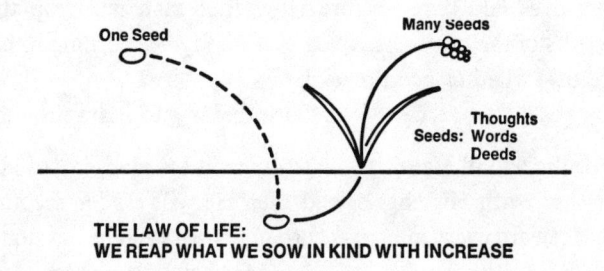

THE LAW OF LIFE: WE REAP WHAT WE SOW IN KIND WITH INCREASE

One Seed → Many Seeds
Seeds: Thoughts, Words, Deeds

If we have sown the weed seeds of:

1. Doubt
2. Despair
3. Hatred
4. Gloom
5. Turmoil
6. Harshness
7. Irritability
8. Moodiness
9. Selfishness
10. Pride
11. Rebellion
12. Resentment
13. Self-pity
14. Criticism
15. Agitation

—we can hardly hope to reap the fine fruit of:

1. Faith	6. Gentleness	11. Temperance
2. Hope	7. Long-suffering	12. Forgiveness
3. Love	8. Faithfulness	13. Compassion
4. Joy	9. Goodness	14. Praise
5. Peace	10. Meekness	15. Rest

When contrasted as above, we see the two lists are typical of the works of the flesh and the fruit of the Spirit, both of which are discussed in the fifth chapter of Galatians. The fruit of the Spirit represents the various qualities which characterize the life of Christ. Every day we are busy both sowing new seed and reaping the harvest of seeds which we have previously sown. Sometimes we reap what we sow immediately; at other times it may take days, months, or even years before the harvest ripens—but reap we shall; if not in full measure in this life, then we most certainly will in the next, where every man will be judged and rewarded according to his works.

> For we must all stand before Christ to be judged and have our lives laid bare—before Him; that each will reap the results of the life he has lived in his body—according to his deeds—whether good or evil.
>
> 2 Corinthians 5:10 (paraphrased)

> For the Son of man is going to come in the glory ... of His Father, with His angels, and then He will render account and reward every man in accordance with what he has done.
>
> Matthew 16:27 AMPLIFIED

The third chapter of First Corinthians deals with the contribution each Christian makes to the household of God—the living Church. It is not a matter of whether we will make a contribution, but what the nature of that contribution will be. Some will offer words and deeds of love, joy, and peace, while others will sow the seeds of criticism, conflict, and condemnation. As we have seen, ultimately there will come a day of reckoning, for we shall surely reap what we have sown—both now and hereafter:

> Everyone's work will be put through the fire so that all can see whether or not it keeps its value. If anyone's work is burned, he shall lose his reward, although like a man leaping through a wall of flame, he himself is saved.
>
> 1 Corinthians 3:13,15 (paraphrased)

If we submit to the purifying flame of God's Holy Spirit now, we need not face the judgment of our works at the coming of Christ, for a burnt-over field is no longer subject to the fire. In fact, such a field is ready to be resown with good seed. Some conservationists believe that fire is nature's way of preparing an area for a healthy period of regrowth. New seedlings can rapidly reproduce without being hindered by either excessive underbrush or overgrowth. Some forest fires have been allowed to burn themselves out with the view that in the long run the results will be biologically most beneficial!

It would be interesting if at the end of each day we could have a rerun by video tape of all of our thoughts, words, and deeds, and then catalog each one in terms of good or bad seed. We could then accurately predict the kind of harvest we might expect for the future—in our lives and others'—for the seed will grow wherever it has been sown. For some of us the flame of God's Spirit might become something to be greatly desired rather than feared, for it would hold the only hope for a renewed life.

Happily, this kind of cleansing is always administered in love, for God never corrects or disciplines as from a motive of retaliation or revenge. Our Heavenly Father is not vindictive, but always desires to reach us redemptively, because He by nature is gracious and full of mercy. Perhaps all of us at this moment might want to pause and deliberately expose our lives to the holy cleansing fire of God's love. Scripture declares that if we confess our sins (every bad seed we have sown in our lives and others') He is faithful and just to forgive us our sins, and *cleanse* us from all unrighteousness (1 John 1:9 paraphrased).

The field of life is now ready to be resown. It might be a meaningful exercise to specifically plan how, where, and with whom we shall begin our project of planting. No farmer would begin the day without knowing what he was going to do. Furthermore, his work of seeding would be done with both faith and expectation. What a thrill it is to see the first green blades break their way through the surface of the soil, for herein is seen a promise for the harvest to come. A golden field of sun-ripened wheat, free from contaminating weeds, is worth working and waiting for.

The life of the field soon becomes the life of the table, and the sowers joyfully break the bread of their labors. The law of the harvest has again been fulfilled, and the workman has reaped the reward of his efforts in the field of life. With thankful hearts we can rejoice in the goodness of our loving Heavenly Father—He is ever faithful to His Word!

> Don't be misled; remember that you can't ignore God and get away with it: a man will always reap just the kind of crop he sows! If he sows to please his own wrong desires, he will be planting seeds of evil and he will surely reap a harvest of spiritual decay and death; but if he plants the good things of the Spirit, he will reap the everlasting life which the Holy Spirit gives him. And let us not get tired of doing what is right, for after a while we will reap a harvest of blessing if we don't get discouraged and give up. That's why whenever we can we should always be kind to everyone, and especially to our Christian brothers.
>
> Galatians 6:7–10 LB

Steady State Controls

As we receive the Bread of Life through the various means available, we shall grow and progressively become stronger in the Lord.

Our ability to resist the stresses and strains in life will likewise increase, and there will come a greater poise and consistency to our walk in the Spirit. There are a variety of "steady-state" mechanisms in a strong healthy body which control the consistency of the internal environment. If we are in a weakened condition through malnutrition, these compensating functions are easily overridden, and we become more susceptible to a variety of disease conditions.

The same is true in the spiritual realm of life. We can expect a balanced diet, spiritually speaking, to contribute to the well-being of our inner man. Our lives will develop an inward stability that enables us to control the changes which come to us through our circumstances, rather than becoming the victims of every unexpected turn of events. That doesn't mean there will not be times when we will be stressed to the limit, but there is a difference between stress and distress. Not all tension is destructive if it is controlled in a positive way.

I was somewhat saddened to learn that physical culturist Charles Atlas had recently passed away, although he was well into his eighties. He was a boyhood hero of mine, for his well-proportioned body gave me a rather lofty ideal towards which to strive. Being a little on the weak and skinny side myself, his magazine advertisements describing his method of "dynamic tension" held an appeal which only someone in my shape could have fully appreciated. Before-and-after pictures of successful students were convincing proof that one really could develop a commanding physique which would discourage the "sand-throwing bullies at the beaches"!

A friend of our family, recognizing a likely candidate when he saw one, gave me the entire Atlas course as a means of encouragement. I was overjoyed and religiously set about putting the program into practice. There was a diversity of instructions concerning nutrition, rest, and other wholesome health habits. The exercises involved the pitting of one muscle group vigorously against another in such a way as to produce a "dynamic tension" designed for developing and strengthening the body. It became very obvious that not all tension, physically speaking, is destructive; when positively controlled it can indeed be very productive—as I was delighted to discover.

Everyone faces a variety of stressing situations and corresponding times of tension as their lot in life. The Adversary of our souls, if not directly responsible for such encounters, will be quick to take advantage of any difficulty which might throw us off balance—spiritually, mentally, emotionally, or physically. Often the arena of conflict involves the close circumstances of our home, church, school, or work. He will not hesitate to engage us in conflict anytime or anywhere, whether we have our gym suit on or not! He does not fight fair, but seeks to throw us for a devastating loss cruelly designed to break our spirit, wrench our souls, and fracture our faith.

Fortunately our Elder Brother is the recognized wrestling Champion of the world! If we will come to His training table and submit to His discipline for our lives, He will carefully program our daily tensions so as to strengthen our faith and build up our inner man. The process may involve some aching muscles and bruised bones, but this is how champions are made. Furthermore, our Trainer automatically becomes our Referee for life, and will not allow our Evil Opponent to press us beyond our endurance. If we faithfully submit to His counsel and loving control, we will wind up "winners" every time, no matter how intense the contest.

> [You] are protected by the power of God through faith for a salvation ready to be revealed in the last time. In this you greatly rejoice, even though now for a little while, if necessary, you have been distressed by various trials, that the proof of your faith, being more precious than gold which is perishable, even though tested by fire, may be found to result in praise and glory and honor at the revelation of Jesus Christ.
>
> 1 Peter 1:5–7 NAS

No temptation has overtaken you but such as is common to man; and God is faithful, who will not allow you to be tempted beyond what you are able; but with the temptation will provide the way of escape also, that you may be able to endure it.

1 Corinthians 10:13 NAS

An Illustration From Life

While writing this chapter I received a phone call that resulted in a counseling session with a lady who had been plagued most of her life with paralyzing fears. She had suffered one nervous breakdown and was apprehensive that, with her tensions in life, she was facing another. I was impressed to share with her that her problems could be traced to three possible sources: a traumatic past, satanic oppression, and/or her own soulish nature. Scarred memories can provoke soulish responses such as resentment, hostility, and self-pity. The devil would be very quick to aggravate such wounds with a chronic infection of like character. In any case, the love of Jesus would be the power which could dispel her fears by reaching to the roots of her problem. He could indeed heal her past, release her from satanic oppression, and enable her to crucify the soulish attitude of persistent pessimism if she were willing to cooperate in faith and follow the total prescription for complete recovery.

God wanted her to know the causes for her problem, the solutions which He had provided, and what her responsibility was in achieving the wholeness she desired. As a daughter in the Father's family who had been filled with the Holy Spirit, she herself possessed the power to resist and overcome the spiritual disease of fear. As we talked and prayed together, the Lord revealed some critical family relationships in the past which had infected her with feelings of being unwanted and unloved. Soulish responses of resentment, jealousy, self-pity, and finally fear had followed. Satan had perniciously fixed these attitudes into her heart and mind as a patterned way of life.

Together in prayer we confessed the healing power which God's love, forgiveness, and compassion were bringing to her mind and memory. We confronted the forces of the Adversary with the Lordship of Jesus Christ through the authority of God's Word and in the power of the Holy Spirit. The "gorilla" was chained, and his hold upon her life was broken! Her husband was called in at this point and together we prayed in the Spirit, joyfully establishing her release and recovery to the glory of God. The dark, furrowed frown on her face gradually gave way to a bright, happy smile, and another lovely hand-maiden of the Lord was on her way to recovery. Life more abundant was now her portion and God's promise, as she would continue to follow the leading of her Good Shepherd and Great Physician—the Lord Jesus Christ. He alone is our guarantee for life with a divine plus.

The Character of Eternal Life

What is the character of eternal life? It can be found in a Person —that Person is Jesus. What determines if one is alive or dead spiritually? The answer lies in the presence or absence of Jesus Christ within our hearts. He *is* LIFE as we were created to live it—forever!

> And the witness is this, that God has given us eternal life, and this life is in His Son. He who has the Son has the life; he who does not have the Son of God does not have the life. These things I have written to you who believe in the name of the Son of God, in order that you may know that you have eternal life.
>
> 1 John 5:11–13 NAS

> The thief comes only to steal, and kill, and destroy; I came that they might have life, and might have it abundantly.
>
> John 10:10 NAS

7
The How of Life

What is the ultimate source of the energy which allows an Indian to start a fire by simply rubbing two sticks together? A perceptive biology student would immediately reply that the sun was that source, and would then proceed to trace the flow of energy and transfer phases involved.

Light energy from the sun is trapped by the photosynthetic process in plants, which convert it into an available form of chemical energy. This energy is stored within the chemical bonds which are formed during the synthesis of plant carbohydrates, proteins, and fats. If a little rabbit should eat a choice meal of green clover, these "plant" components would then be converted into "rabbit" carbohydrate, protein, and fat through the process of digestion and assimilation. (There is a sense in which rabbits are nothing more than "processed clover"!) Some of these organic nutrients would also be "burned" as fuel to energize the life functions of the rabbit. Such transfer phases are never one-hundred percent efficient, however, and much energy is lost in the form of radiant heat.

Should our Indian friend catch and eat the little rabbit, the energy stored in "rabbit" carbohydrate, protein, and fat would become "Indian" energy as these organic nutrients were utilized for the synthesis of new tissue—or "burned" for the release of energy required to flex the muscles involved in rubbing two sticks together. Chemical energy would thus be transformed into mechanical energy which would produce the heat of friction at a sufficient level to ignite the sticks. Chemical energy bound in the plant-produced sticks would then be converted into the heat and light of combustion, which is immediately radiated into space.

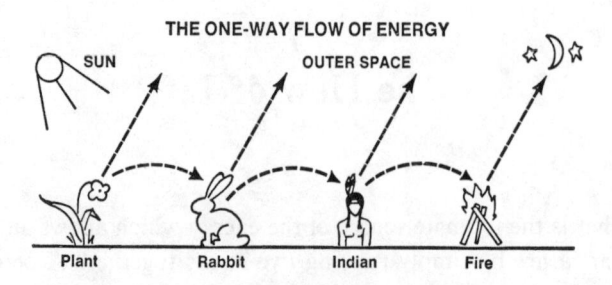

THE ONE-WAY FLOW OF ENERGY

Plant　　Rabbit　　Indian　　Fire

The Perpetual Need for Power

It is obvious in this intricate but interesting sequence of events that no energy can be self-generated apart from the sun. Furthermore, in the transfer of energy from one form and phase to another, it is continually being dissipated as either heat or light, and eventually will be forever lost in outer space. A perpetual input of power from the sun is necessary or the metabolic wheels of life would slowly grind to a halt, never to turn again. No wonder God said at the very beginning of Creation let there be light (radiant energy); and with the word went the energizing power of God's Spirit—and there was light!

Anything that blocks the vital flow of energy through an organism will lessen or completely extinguish the flame of life. The weakening effects of "tired blood" (anemia) are due to a decrease in the oxygen-carrying capacity of the red blood cells. Without oxygen, the energy-releasing process of respiration is hindered, and we continually feel tired and are easily worn out. There just isn't enough energy being produced to turn the wheels of our metabolic machinery rapidly enough to keep us running in the race of life as we should.

An even more dramatic illustration of the necessity for energy transmission is the drastic effects of cyanide gas. This is the chemical used in the death chamber, where deadly fumes arise after a pellet falls into a container of acid. It takes only a matter of seconds for the cyanide gas to reach vital cell reactions by way of the bloodstream. Cyanide acts quickly to stop the power-releasing process of respiration by blocking essential enzymes at the cellular level. All the cells in the body simultaneously cease their production of energy, and death is instantaneous. Yes, a continuous flow of energy is absolutely essential for the existence of natural life.

Should the light of the sun suddenly be extinguished, not only would the earth be plunged into darkness, but the reservoirs of available energy would soon be depleted, and our world would slowly succumb to the still, silent slumber of death—never to be awakened again! These poetic words of Job take on an added meaning when considered from the above scientific perspective:

> Truly the light is sweet, and a pleasant thing it is for the eyes to behold the sun.
>
> Ecclesiastes 11:7 AMPLIFIED

Divine Provision for Spiritual Power

Just as there must be a continual supply of radiant energy from the sun with regard to the economy of natural life, so our life in the Lord requires a perpetual flow of spiritual power for its existence. The source of this divine energy must be from above, for we can no more generate spiritual power on our own than a green plant can exist apart from the sun. God alone is the source of the divine power which motivates our Christian life. For this reason He has sent to us His Holy Spirit.

> For you shall receive power after the Holy Spirit has come upon you; and you shall be my witnesses both in Jerusalem and in all Judea and Samaria, and even to the ends of the earth.
>
> Acts 1:8 (paraphrased)

The Greek term for power in the above passage is "dunamis," from which we derive our English words *dynamic, dynamo,* and *dynamite.* It refers to the ability or force which resides in something, and the exertion of that force—power in action. The thought also conveys the idea of power which produces a change as a result of its performance.

The corresponding Hebrew word for power is "koach." It is found, for instance, in this familiar passage from the prophets:

> ... Not by might, nor by power, but by my spirit, saith the LORD of hosts.
>
> Zechariah 4:6

Man does not have within himself the power to change himself or his world for God's greater purpose: therefore our Heavenly Father has promised us the presence and power of His Holy Spirit.

It was the Spirit of God which moved (hovered, brooded) over the face of the waters when the earth was yet without form and void and darkness was upon the face of the deep. A formless, lightless, and lifeless world was overshadowed by the creative power of God's Holy Spirit. Then God spoke. With His Word went His Spirit, and light flashed into existence; the heavens and the earth found their fashion; and life in all of its diversity filled a still, silent world with sound and movement. And God saw that it was very good (Genesis 1)!

Creation is a beautiful example of divine power with purpose. As discussed earlier, man was set upon the scene with the commission to fill the earth with loyal, loving sons and daughters who would increasingly express the divine life of their Lord and Creator. Satan sought to spoil God's glorious plan by infecting man with the sin of rebellion. The outcome would have been a timeless tragedy if God had not in grace planted into His original Creation the seeds of redemptive purpose.

Once more the life-giving breath of God hastens to bring renewed life to a waiting world which spiritually speaking is lightless, lifeless, and without form. Again God speaks, but this time the Living Word will be clothed in flesh, and the redeeming power of God will walk

His way across the earth that all men might know the joy of restored fellowship with their Father-Creator. A new creation is under way, and true to divine pattern, it begins with the brooding power of the life-giving Spirit of God:

> Then the angel said to Mary, the Holy Spirit will come *upon* you and the power of the Most High will *overshadow* you; therefore the child to be born will be called holy, the Son of God.
>
> Luke 1:35 (paraphrased)

The "Light and Life" of the world was to come "fashioned" in the form of flesh that He might in every respect be a real Brother-Redeemer. In His death we find redemption; in His life we find our example of divine life as we were created to live it.

The Heavenly Secret to Earthly Success

What is the secret to a successful life here on earth as Jesus lived it? Through Him the full will and purpose of the Father was fulfilled, and this is our calling too! What was the motivating power which sustained His daily life, supported Him in death, and ultimately was the reason for His Resurrection? The Scripture gives us the answer:

> And the Spirit of the Lord shall rest *upon* him, the Spirit of wisdom, understanding, counsel and might; the Spirit of knowledge and of the fear of the Lord. His delight will be obedience to the Lord. . . . he will be *clothed* with fairness and with truth.
>
> Isaiah 11:2-5 LB (italics mine)

And the Holy Spirit descended *upon* Him in bodily form, like a dove, and a voice came from heaven saying, You are My beloved *Son* in whom I am well pleased. . . . Then Jesus went back full of and under the *power* of the Holy Spirit to

Galilee. ... And they were amazed at His teaching, for His word was with *authority* and *power*. ... With *authority* and *power* He commands the foul spirits, and they come out!
Luke 3:22; 4:1, 14, 36 (paraphrased)

And Jesus came and spake unto them, saying, All *power* [authority] is given unto me in heaven and in earth.
Matthew 28:18 (italics mine)

... God anointed Jesus of Nazareth with the Holy Ghost and with *power:* who went about doing good, and healing all that were oppressed of the devil; for God was with him.
Acts 10:38 (italics mine)

Jesus was aware that in His humanity He was totally dependent upon the power of the Holy Spirit. Furthermore, He carefully instructed His disciples that after His departure they too would need that power to fulfill their commission as His witnesses to a world that was under the dominion of darkness.

As the Father has sent Me, even so send I you. And when He had said this, He breathed on them and said, Receive the Holy Spirit.... And behold, I send forth the promise of My Father *upon* you: but tarry in the city of Jerusalem until you are *clothed* with *power* from on high, for you shall receive *power* after that the Holy Spirit has come *upon* you!
John 20:21, 22; Luke 24:49; Acts 1:8 (paraphrased)

Behold, I give unto you *power* [authority] to tread on serpents and scorpions, and over all the power of the enemy: and nothing shall by any means hurt you.
Luke 10:19

On the day of Pentecost the promise was *fulfilled,* as they were *infilled* with the Holy Spirit and with power to praise and proclaim the reality of their risen Lord.

And when the day of Pentecost was fully come, they were all with one accord in one place. And suddenly there came a sound from heaven as of a rushing *mighty* wind . . . And there appeared unto them cloven tongues like as of fire, and it sat *upon* each of them. And they were all filled with the Holy Ghost, and began to speak with other tongues . . . the wonderful works of God . . . as the Spirit gave them utterance.

Acts 2:1–4, 11

It is of interest to note that the little word "upon" when associated with the coming of the Holy Spirit is rather consistently associated with a divine commission of power and authority. This is seen in the above passages concerning Christ's earthly ministry. The descending Dove of God's Spirit rests "upon" Him, and Jesus decisively moves forth to establish the rule and reign of His Father's Kingdom here on earth as it is in heaven. Demon power withers under the authority of His Word; the gates of hell are shaken by the power of His mighty works; death is deprived of its sting, and the grave gives way to Resurrection glory!

Then Jesus informs His disciples just prior to His Ascension that as the Father had sent Him, so He was sending them as witnesses into the world—but only after they had also been "clothed" from on high with the power of God's Holy Spirit. This was to be the secret of their success!

Commissioned by the King

We are included in Christ's commission to go forth into all the world with the good news of God's redeeming love. The full meaning of the word "witness" is far more than just words but involves the total testimony of our very lives themselves. We are to become the light of God's love to a world that has been wounded by the violence and injustice of our day. Only the government of God, in the form of His Kingdom, can provide the healing and proclaim the peace which is so desperately needed in this hour. His royal reign begins in the hearts of His loyal people who wish to bring a bright ray of hope in a darkening day by heralding the coming of Christ as King. The redeeming rule of our Kingly Brother can begin now, as God's people confront evil in our world with the good news of the Gospel. And it is a Gospel which requires a sense of responsibility on the part of its proclaimers, for it is a proclamation in deed as well as in word. Our whole life is to be a witness to the whole world—and this involves every arena of experience, as discussed in an earlier chapter.

For some of us a destiny so demanding and daring is more of a discouragement than it is an incentive, for our own weakness and lack of preparation leave us feeling most inadequate—maybe even inferior. I once had a pastor who, because of his military background, presented every aspect (or so it struck me) of our life in Christ as a vigorous war of aggression in which we were to be bold, brave soldiers of the cross—mighty champions of the truth. Every member of the church was to be a terrifying "tiger" Christian, making marvelous leaps of faith as we would boldly bound from one glorious victory to another. I had some difficulty relating to the "tiger" image, because I frankly featured myself more as a "bunny rabbit"—who never could get his tiger skin on straight!

Although this analogy may be somewhat exaggerated (although painfully accurate on occasions), it does bring into focus two truths. First of all, in God's family zoo there is a place for both rabbits and tigers (as well as lambs and lions). They are not to compete, but complement each other in character. Some by nature and divine gifts are more aggressive and daring in their endeavors; others are more reflective and soft-spoken in their ministry. The character and personality of the evangelist and prophet will differ from that of pastor and teacher, but both are needed.

Secondly, neither the tiger nor the rabbit can fully express his nature and purpose in the economy of life if he is in a weakened or crippled condition because of hunger, thirst, or accident. Many Christians feel they are disabled and powerless when confronted with what seems to be the overwhelming demands of our Christian life and witness. Each new challenge to "rise up and go forth to battle" merely emphasizes their inadequacy and feelings of inferiority. The inner yearning and longing of their hearts to be strong and whole in the eyes of God and their fellow Christians is increased.

Provisions for Power

It is difficult for a weak and wounded individual to feel he is really wanted, loved, and accepted. If we always seem to fall short of the standard of the "model Christian," how much in our life is really all that desirable, lovable, or even respectable in the view of anyone— God included? How comforting are the words of our wonderful Lord —He who is touched by the feelings of our infirmities—when He sympathetically declares that it is not the healthy who need a physician, but those who are sick (Luke 5:31). Jesus Christ, as our Great Physician, desires to heal the broken hearts and restore the wounded souls of His beloved brothers and sisters. As our Great Provider, He Himself would become for us the "bread and water" of life!

> Blessed are they which hunger and thirst after righteousness (right standing—an acceptable position) for they shall be filled (completely satisfied).
>
> Matthew 5:6 (paraphrased)

> ... Jesus stood forth and cried in a loud voice, If any man is *thirsty,* let him come to Me and drink! He who believes in Me ... as the Scripture has said, Out from his innermost being springs and rivers of living water shall *flow* (continuously). But He was speaking here of the Holy Spirit, Whom those who believed ... in Him were afterward to receive. For the Holy Spirit had not yet been given; because Jesus was not yet glorified. ...
>
> *See* John 7:37–39 AMPLIFIED

But whoever takes a drink of the water that I will give him shall never, no never, be thirsty any more. But the water that I will give him shall become a spring of water welling up (flowing, bubbling) continually within him (into, for) eternal life.

See John 4:14 AMPLIFIED

These passages from John's Gospel present a refreshing picture of what is promised to those who will listen with faith to the voice of the Lord. With great feeling Jesus calls and invites those who are thirsty to come to Him and drink deeply from the fountain of living water.

The different streams of the Holy Spirit speak of the various gifts, graces, and fruit of the Spirit which enable us to fully express the life of Jesus. As white light is broken up into the rainbow colors of the spectrum by a prism, so our lives are to transmit the various qualities of Christ's character and life in a bright display of His glory. To exclude any of God's gifts or graces from our lives would leave us with a spectrum without the full range of color. Both God's power and purpose is thereby limited in our lives, individually and corporately, as His representatives here on earth.

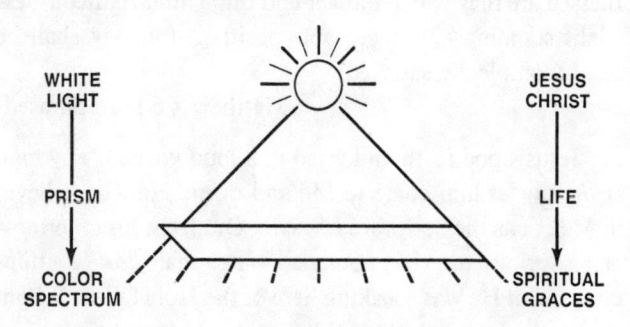

The Fruit of the Spirit

The fruit of the Spirit is grown in our lives as we submit to the character-producing ministry of the Holy Spirit within us. The typical list found in Galatians 5:22–23 describes the character or "being" of Jesus, into whose image we are to be conformed. It is interesting to study the various fruits of the Spirit as expressions of His life:

The Rainbow Colors of Divine Character

Love	Being Lovely
Joy	Being Joyful
Peace	Being Peaceful
Long-suffering	Being Patient
Gentleness	Being Kind
Goodness	Being Benevolent
Faith	Being Faithful
Meekness	Being Humble
Temperance	Being Self-controlled

The various fruits of the Spirit are grown best from the ground of contrary circumstances. When the Apostle Paul complained concerning his thorn in the flesh, the Lord informed him that from the "ground" of his *weakness* would come forth the "fruit" of God's *strength* (2 Corinthians 12:9). Paul picked up the principle, for the same concept is conveyed throughout his epistles:

> We can rejoice, too, when we run into problems and trials for we know that they are good for us—they help us learn to be patient. And patience develops strength of character in us and helps us trust God more each time we use it until finally our hope and faith are strong and steady. Then, when that happens, we are able to hold our heads high no matter what happens and know that all is well, for we know how dearly God loves us, and we feel this warm love everywhere within us because God has given us the Holy Spirit to fill our hearts with his love.
>
> Romans 5:3–5 LB

The concept that the finest fruit grows from the ground of contrary circumstances is summarized in the following diagram:

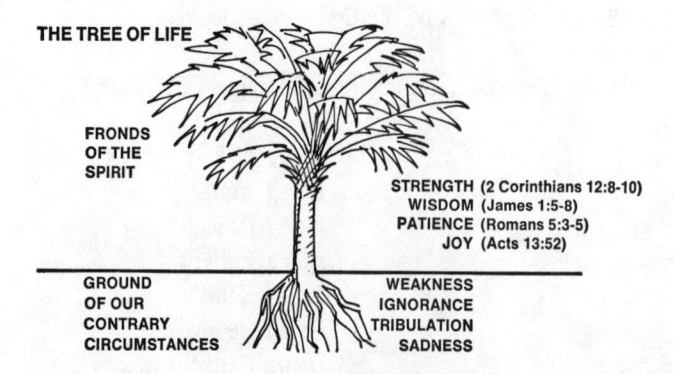

THE TREE OF LIFE

FRONDS OF THE SPIRIT

STRENGTH (2 Corinthians 12:8-10)
WISDOM (James 1:5-8)
PATIENCE (Romans 5:3-5)
JOY (Acts 13:52)

GROUND OF OUR CONTRARY CIRCUMSTANCES

WEAKNESS
IGNORANCE
TRIBULATION
SADNESS

Recently I attended the Eighth International Catholic Charismatic Conference, where I had been invited to be one of the speakers for the Sunday afternoon celebration in the football stadium of Notre Dame University. After arriving on campus the preceding Friday, I made the irritating discovery that I had neglected to pack my toothbrush, in spite of my checklist personally designed to prevent just such catastrophes. After running out of Dentyne chewing gum Saturday afternoon, I decided I should stop by the local bookstore and purchase a toothbrush. To my dismay, long waiting lines extended behind every checkout counter. Conference participants had converged upon the little store to pick up souvenir items to take home with them.

After picking up a 69-cent toothbrush, I crowded my way back to the end of the line which I thought was making the best progress. Careful calculations with my wristwatch determined that I was in for a thirty- or forty-minute wait. I prayed that another counter might miraculously open up and God would graciously show His mercy upon me. I was tired, and needed to come apart from the crowds and restfully and peacefully wait upon Him for my presentation for Sunday afternoon. What actually happened was that my line seemed to slow down in comparison with the others, which only added fuel to my fires of impatience and resentment.

I finally realized that God might have a higher purpose than providing for my creature comforts. I was informed there was no reason He could not inspire my thoughts for the Sunday meeting right on the spot. One of the themes might relate to our need for patiently waiting upon Him as He wisely arranges the affairs for our lives—and the world. I was also reminded that the fruits of the Spirit were actually attributes of God's nature and when grown within our lives possessed an eternal quality—something that would last forever. To impatiently save a few moments in time can be at the expense of eternal gain! Very clearly, the fruit of the Spirit provides us with the "growing" power which is needed to conform our lives into the character of our Model and Elder Brother, the Lord Jesus Christ.

The Gifts of the Spirit

The gifts of the Spirit are presented to us by the Apostle Paul in the twelfth chapter of First Corinthians, and further discussed in the thirteenth and fourteenth chapters. From a study of the Greek terms translated "gift," and from the context in which they are found, it is apparent that these expressions of the Holy Spirit are:

Spiritual	not psychological
Supernatural	not natural
Gifts	not rewards
Timely	not permanent

A spiritual gift, therefore, may be defined as a supernatural capacity or power *specifically* expressed through a believer that God's will might be realized for a *particular* time, place, people, and purpose.

As the fruit of the Spirit enables us to develop the "character" of Christ (His *being*), so the gifts of the Spirit allow us to approach His likeness in:

Concept   His *thinking*
Conversation   His *speaking*
Conduct   His *doing*

in particular times of specific need. This approach allows us to classify and define each gift in the following fashion:

The Gifts of the Spirit (1 Corinthians 12:8-10)

A. DISCERNING GIFTS (THOUGHT)
Gifts of Revelation: *Power to Know*

1. *A word of wisdom:*
   A divinely given directive concerning a course of action or a conversational response through which the will of God can be realized in a specific situation (Matthew 22:21; Luke 12:12; Acts 15:13-31).

2. *A word of knowledge:*
   A divinely given insight into God's will and/or man's condition which otherwise would not be known by the natural mind (John 4:17-19; Acts 5:19; 1 Corinthians 13:2).

3. *Discerning of spirits:*
   A divinely given power of perception by which the motivating source of inspiration behind an individual is determined —whether it be of God, man, or Satan (1 Corinthians 14:29; Acts 16:16-18).

B. DECLARATION GIFTS (WORD)
Gifts of Utterance: *Power to Speak*

1. *Prophecy:*
   Divinely inspired utterance which can involve both *foretelling* (prediction) and *forth-telling* (edification—building up; comfort—cheering up; exhortation—stirring up). Its pur-

pose is to convict the unbeliever and edify the saints (Acts 20:23, 21:4, 10–11; 1 Corinthians 14:3, 24–25).

2. *Various kinds of tongues:*
Divinely prompted utterance composed of sounds and syllables unknown to the mind of the speaker but permeated with spiritual purpose and power. When expressed in a meeting, this gift unites the hearts of God's people and prepares them to receive the interpretation. The supernatural dimension associated with this gift may serve as a "sign" to the unbeliever (1 Corinthians 14:2, 13–14, 22).

3. *Interpretation of tongues:*
Divinely inspired response to the previous manifestation of tongues which is spoken in a language understood by the listeners. It may be a warm expression of praise to the Lord, or an edifying revelation from God's heart and mind for His people (1 Corinthians 14:5, 6, 15).

C. DYNAMIC GIFTS (DEED)
Gifts of Power: *Power to Do*

1. *Faith:*
A divine impartation of certainty for a given situation which is beyond the limitations of both sense and reason. This gift provides an inner assurance which for the moment excludes the possibility of doubt (Hebrews 11:1; Matthew 21:21; Acts 3:4–9, 16).

2. *Gifts of healing:*
A divine ministry of restoring power for physical and psychological infirmities. The word "healing" used here has the connotation of *wholeness* for spirit, soul, and body, yet with a sense of specificity—each gift specially suited for divine purpose in a personal way (Mark 16:17, 18; Acts 28:8, 9).

3. *Working of miracles:*
A divine manifestation of wonder-working power apart from healings that may involve creative activity—multiplication of the loaves and fishes, new organs, resurrection from the dead. Also involved would be phenomena beyond the explanation of natural laws—walking on the water, changing water to wine, multiplication of bread and fish. (There have been many testimonies of similar modern-day miracles.) Other demonstrations of miracle power would include: demonic deliverance, protection (in God's will) from poison and serpents, and speaking unlearned earthly languages (Mark 16:17-20; Acts 2:8-11; 19:11-12; 28:1-6).

The above list of spiritual gifts is undoubtedly typical and not intended to be all-inclusive. Furthermore, many of the gifts probably overlap in function and are expressed in concert with each other. They are, however, specific in terms of time, place, and purpose: they are particular manifestations, not general or universal ministries.

General Ministries of the Holy Spirit

Besides the *specific* "gifts" outlined above, there is a scriptural basis for describing corresponding *general* "ministries" of the Holy Spirit which are similar in character to the gifts but differ in that they are more universal in their expression and develop in line with our spiritual maturity.

For instance, besides the "gift" of faith, which operates on specific occasions only, there is the general "attitude" or "ministry" of faith which motivates our daily walk, and without which it is impossible to please God (Hebrews 11:6). Likewise, the "gift" of tongues is for the edification of the Body of Christ when followed by the "gift" of interpretation, but Paul makes it very clear that there is also a private prayer tongue or language which can be expressed at will for our edification in Christ. With it our prayer, petitions, intercessions, and praise are lifted beyond the limitations of our natural minds and ever presented in harmony with God's will and pleasure (1 Corinthians 14).

From these examples it becomes apparent that the "general" ministries of the Spirit are for everyone, all the time, everywhere, and are designed to bring stability and strength to our daily life in the Spirit. They may be outlined following the same pattern as for the "gifts" of the Spirit.

A. MINISTRIES OF REVELATION

1. *Knowledge:*
   A ministry of progressive revelation by which we discover the answers to the "what" and "why" questions concerning God's will and plan (Ephesians 1:17–18; Colossians 1:9–10; 1 Corinthians 2).

2. *Wisdom:*
   A ministry of progressive revelation by which we discover the answers to the "how," "when," "where," and "who" questions concerning God's will and plan (James 1:5; 1 Corinthians 2).

3. *Discernment:*
   A ministry of progressive revelation by which we understand the principles of spiritual judgment in our Christian walk (Matthew 16:3; Hebrews 5:14).

B. MINISTRIES OF UTTERANCE

1. *Tongues:*
   A ministry of divinely inspired prayer and praise for our private devotions wherein we may be lifted beyond the limitations of our reason and emotions (1 Corinthians 14:2, 4, 15–19).

2. *Interpretation:*
   A ministry of inspired enlightenment following our praying

in tongues wherein our minds are renewed that our prayer and praise in our native tongue will more accurately reflect the will and pleasure of God (Romans 12:2; 1 Corinthians 2: 9–16; Ephesians 6:18; Jude 20).

3. *Prophecy:*
A ministry of inspired speech which will energize our witnessing, counselling, preaching, and teaching, that others may hear something of Jesus when they listen to our words (Acts 4:8, 29–31; 6:10).

C. MINISTRIES OF POWER

1. *Faith:*
A ministry of positive thinking whereby our inner attitude will reflect the hope and confidence we have in the faithfulness of God's Word, God's Son, and God's Spirit (Hebrews 11:6; Romans 10:17; Hebrews 12:2).

2. *Healings:*
A ministry of divine health as a daily confession of faith and thanksgiving for God's care and protection (Exodus 15:26; Proverbs 4:20–22; 3 John 2).

3. *Miracles:*
A ministry of expectation wherein all of our walk with God is seen as a miracle of His grace. Supernatural touches of His protecting and directing hand are recognized with praise and thanksgiving (Romans 8:14, 28; Acts 17:28).

One could think of the specific gifts as waves which momentarily break forth from the rising tide of the general ministries of the Holy Spirit. As the general ministries mature in our lives, the more effective will become the specific gifts, for they will arise from a life which has a consistency in character. The fruits of the Spirit are closely associated with the general ministries because both are continually contributing to our Christian stature.

Fruit and Gifts: Complementary Expressions of God's Grace

As implied above, the specific gifts of the Spirit are not necessarily marks of maturity or measurements of Christian character as are the fruit and general ministries of the Spirit. It takes time and testing to grow in grace; the "gifts," on the other hand, are sovereignly given to those who will seek after them in faith and obedience (1 Corinthians 12:7, 11; 14:1, 12). It also takes time to learn to "excel" in the gifts, but this is because the excellence of expression must be coupled with the fruit of the Spirit. Without the *fruit* of love, the *gifts* of tongues, prophecy, knowledge, faith, et cetera will never call forth God's approval or recognition upon one's ministry. Paul never depreciated any of the *gifts,* but he does declare that without love the "gifted" *person* is a cipher in God's record book (1 Corinthians 13:2-3). Perhaps this is the reason Christ said there would be some who would cry, "Lord, Lord did we not prophesy, cast out devils, and do many wonderful works [miracles of power] in thy name?"—but He would reply that He had never known (recognized) them on earth, nor could such an "empty" life now find reward in the Heavenly Kingdom. This evaluation by the Lord is not surprising, for earlier in His discussion He indicated that it is by one's "fruits" that his life and ministry will be measured (Matthew 7:15-23).

On the positive side, a life and ministry that display the full complement of both God's gifts and His graces will gain His full approval. The fruit and gifts were never intended to be placed in competition with one another, for neither can find full expression without the other. The gifts of the Spirit actually are "love gifts"—provisions by which God conveys His love to our specific needs and fulfills His divine purpose in and through our lives.

When I was a boy I took piano lessons for one year. At the end of that time it seemed best for all concerned that the endeavor be brought to a conclusion. I did learn some elementary things, however, about playing the piano. For instance, it is necessary for *both* the right and left hands to strike the proper notes to produce chords that harmonize with each other. (That was my basic problem.) When properly executed, numerous chord combinations are possible which provide many different variations for a given theme. This presents a perfect picture of the way the fruit and gifts of the Spirit are to be selectively harmonized in our lives that the perfect will of our Heavenly Father can be forthcoming for our good and His glory. God has wisely and graciously provided us with a continual source of power through the everflowing streams of His Spirit, whereby we can become like His Son and find our function in His family as beloved sons and daughters.

In summary, we can refer to the following diagram, which depicts both our life and power relationship with Jesus as Saviour and Baptizer. Through the fruit and gifts of the Spirit we become like Jesus in both our character and conduct, and are likewise prepared for our ministry in the family of God.

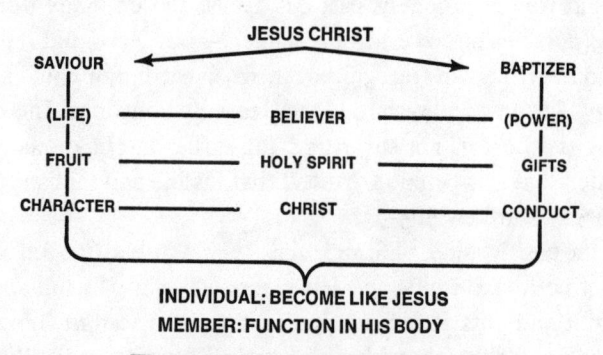

```
                    JESUS CHRIST
        SAVIOUR ←——————————————→ BAPTIZER
          |                          |
         (LIFE) ———— BELIEVER ———— (POWER)
          |                          |
         FRUIT ———— HOLY SPIRIT ———— GIFTS
          |                          |
      CHARACTER ———— CHRIST ———— CONDUCT
          └──────────────┬──────────────┘
           INDIVIDUAL: BECOME LIKE JESUS
           MEMBER: FUNCTION IN HIS BODY
```

The Father's Promise Fulfilled

Several years ago following an interfaith charismatic worship service, a Catholic sister expressed a desire to inquire further concerning the gifts of the Spirit. There had been a beautiful spontaneity in praise, prayer, and worship as the Holy Spirit had graciously bestowed many of His gifts upon the meeting. She had warmly responded to the lovely presence of the Lord in our midst, but had many questions of a specific nature.

She was the principal of the school where the meeting had been held, and was garbed in the flowing habit of her order. As we seated ourselves at the front of the now empty auditorium, she spoke both directly and sincerely: "I have responded to the love and warmth of the worship, but some aspects of the meeting were quite different from my experience and tradition." She had heard, in some of the personal testimonies, references to the reality of a heavenly prayer language—the privilege of praying in an unknown tongue. "Now this is something I know very little about," she confided, "and I am not altogether sure it is even anything in which I would be interested."

I suggested that rather than beginning with a gift of the Spirit, a spiritual experience, or even the Holy Spirit Himself, we should start with the Person of Jesus Christ and see everything related to Him. She warmly responded, and I sensed that Jesus was a very near and dear friend of hers whom she deeply loved. We talked about the eternal heart desire of the Father that we become like His Son in character, conversation, and conduct, and honestly confessed our own weakness and frustration in attempting to achieve such a noble ideal by our own grit, wit, and determination. We then shared how the promised Comforter had come to be our constant companion and friend who by His power and through His gifts and graces could lift us beyond our limitations. His desire was to fulfill the will of the Father by wisely, lovingly, and faithfully revealing, realizing, and releasing Jesus—to, in, and through us—thereby conforming us unto His image!

The fruits of the Spirit were considered as qualities of Christ's character, while the gifts were recognized as supernatural abilities by which His thoughts, words, and works could be decisively expressed for a specific purpose in God's will. These various expressions of the Spirit were seen as provisions for all believers who in faith would claim the full power and presence of the Holy Spirit in their lives.

It was understood in salvation that the Holy Spirit indeed *indwelt* us as the life of Christ, but that we all also needed to be *filled to overflowing* as well. Our part was to pray for the full provision of God's Spirit, to appropriate the promise in faith, and as patterned throughout the Book of Acts, enabling us to joyfully respond to His presence with a divine language of heavenly praise. The latter response on our part would be an active expression of faith, love, obedience, and humility. The very power that could tame our tongue —our most unruly member—could also rule our lives for His holy purpose in an unholy world. How wise of the Lord to have chosen to confirm our faith in the fullness of His Spirit by conferring a gift which represents His sovereign power. No longer is the intellect enshrined on the altar of life, but now is brought to a place of submission that God's Spirit might rule and reign supreme. The Tree of Life rather than the Tree of Knowledge thus finds its rightful place of preeminence in the interior garden of our soul.

From this fountain of freedom in worship springs a diversity of spiritual graces which always follow in the wake of an active, living faith. No longer is the Book of Acts a dusty document recording the relics of once-mighty works which long since have disappeared from the hope and history of the church. The finger of God's Spirit continues to write words of life and perform works of grace wherever His loving sons and daughters are willing to reach forth in faith.

At this point a beloved daughter of God, and my sister in Christ, expressed her desire for everything in His Spirit which God had provided for her. She had walked closely with her Lord, but recognized her lack of power to fully express His life in her religious vocation. There was a loving concern in her heart for the children under her charge that they would come to know and feel the presence of God in their daily lives. Beyond the academic aim of her profession was the greater goal of bringing young lives to a place of commitment to their Lord. Leading little children to their place in the Father's family brings an overwhelming sense of responsibility which demands the full power of God's gifts and graces. There was also the desire to worship the Lord from the wellsprings of her soul, as did Mary, the model handmaiden of the Lord, at the time of the Annunciation.

As we bowed our heads in prayer, she softly praised the Lord for the many years it had been her privilege to know and serve Him. The need for greater power in her life, and the desire to freely praise and worship God, were honestly confessed. We reverently but expectantly requested that our Heavenly Father would fulfill His promise concerning the fullness of His Spirit for one of His own dear daughters whose life had been laid before Him in love. In simplicity she also yielded her life to her Elder Brother, the Lord Jesus, that she might personally experience a beautiful baptism into the ever-flowing river of God's Holy Spirit.

While we were praying, the gentle Dove of Heaven graciously touched her life, bringing the warm witness of His infilling presence. Her Blessed Comforter had come to draw her into closer communion with Himself than she had ever known before. His Holy Presence filled her soul with praise, and I simply suggested that she join with me, that together we might magnify the name of the Lord. A lovely language of inspired praise formed upon her lips and was offered up as sweet incense before the Holy Altar of God.

It was one of those occasions where the presence of the Lord was so real it could be felt. We both responded with an overwhelming sense of holy joy. Little phrases from Scripture, like "the oil of gladness," "the joy of the Lord," "filled with joy and the Holy Spirit," take on a freshness in meaning after personally experiencing such a time of "holy hilarity" in the Lord. Far from fanaticism, such joy, the Word declares, is to be the source of our strength (Nehemiah 8:10).

Joyless Christians are weak, anemic Christians; and weak, anemic Christians are joyless Christians! Very obviously, one of the secrets to a consistently energetic Christian life will be an abiding joy in the Lord. It was this joy into which we both had been freshly immersed. What began as a serious conversation about the gifts of the Holy Spirit joyfully concluded with a personal experience with the Giver Himself. Once again the Father had faithfully fulfilled His promise! (Reading suggestion for those interested in the significance and simplicity of personally appropriating the "Father's Promise": *Aglow With the Spirit,* by Robert C. Frost, published by Logos International.)

Life's Greatest Discovery

No better conclusion could be drawn from the pages of this little book concerning life's basic questions than that the answers are to be discovered in the Person of the Lord Jesus Christ Himself:

> As our REDEEMER-BROTHER, He restores divine meaning and purpose to our vain and wasted lives through His great work of salvation. *In Him we have discovered the "why" of Life.*
>
> As our MODEL-BROTHER, He provides us with the perfect pattern for life as we were created to live it. *In Him we have discovered the "what" of Life.*
>
> As our ROYAL BROTHER, He confers upon us a kingly commission which provides us with a personal dignity and a princely destiny. *In Him we have discovered the "who" of Life.*
>
> As our BAPTIZER-BROTHER He invests us with spiritual power and authority by which our heavenly commission can be fulfilled. *In Him we have discovered the "how" of Life.*
>
> As our ETERNAL BROTHER, He synchronizes our daily lives with the timeless heartbeat and desire of the Everlasting Father. *In Him we have discovered the "when" of Life.*
>
> As our SHEPHERD-BROTHER, He faithfully leads us in paths of righteousness here on earth that we might live together in the family of our Heavenly Father forever. *In Him we have discovered the "where" of Life.*

FOR ME TO LIVE IS CHRIST!